HANDBOOK ON MICROGRIDS FOR POWER QUALITY AND CONNECTIVITY

JULY 2020

ASIAN DEVELOPMENT BANK

ADB

Notes:
In this publication, "$" refers to United States dollars.
ADB recognizes "China" as the People's Republic of China.

Cover design by Kookie Triviño.

Photo credits on the cover, clockwise from left:

Transmission lines: Energy Sector Development Investment Program in Afghanistan (photo by Jawad Jalali); Wind
farm: 150-Megawatt Burgos Wind Farm Project in the Philippines (ADB); Battery: Solar-Wind Hybrid Project site in
Pakistan (photo by Nasr ur Rahman); Light bulb: Power Transmission and Distribution Project in Afghanistan (ADB);
Electric tricycle: Mitigation of Climate Change through Increased Energy Efficiency and the Use of Clean Energy in the
Philippines (ADB); Controller: Solar Minigrid Pilot Project in Nepal (photo by C. Lao Torregosa).

Contents

Tables, Figures, and Boxes

Boxes

Foreword

This *Handbook on Microgrids for Power Quality and Connectivity* is part of a series of reference materials on advanced technologies. The objectives of this series are to support the Asian Development Bank (ADB) operations in adopting and deploying advanced technologies in energy projects for its developing member countries, scale up the ADB Clean Energy Program, and bring the energy sector closer to achieving its targets in climate finance.

Developed countries are implementing large-scale smart grid technologies. Many developing countries are also in the process of adopting various smart grid components into their power systems. Microgrids as one type of distributed energy systems with various renewables and smart grid components can connect and disconnect from the conventional main grid as physical and/or economic conditions dictate, to enable it to operate in either grid-connected mode (synchronous with the grid) or island mode (functioning autonomously and disconnected from the main electric grid).

Microgrids have a critical role in transforming energy systems as a novel distribution network architecture within the broader smart grids concept that will contribute to the energy 5Ds—decentralization, decarbonization, digitalization, decreasing consumption, disintermediation. We hope that this handbook serves as a helpful reference for ADB operations and its developing member countries as we collectively face the daunting task at hand.

Yongping Zhai
Chief of Energy Sector Group
Asian Development Bank

Acknowledgments

The *Handbook on Microgrids for Power Quality and Connectivity* is an output of a comprehensive study carried out by the Sustainable Development and Climate Change Department (SDCC) of the Asian Development Bank (ADB) under Regional Technical Assistance 9690: Integrated High Impact Innovation in Sustainable Energy Technology–Energy System Analysis, Technology Road Maps, and Feasibility Studies for Pilot Testing.

The study was conducted by a team in the Sector Advisory Service Cluster–Energy Sector Group led by Susumu Yoneoka, energy specialist, under the overall guidance of Robert Guild, chief sector officer, and Yongping Zhai, chief of the Energy Sector Group. Two international experts were also part of the team and made invaluable contributions in their capacities as authors of background papers.

This handbook was written by Susumu Yoneoka and consultants Sasank Goli and Sagar Gubbi. Kee-Yung Nam, principal energy economist, SDCC, reviewed the publication structure. Charity L. Torregosa, senior energy officer, coordinated the production and worked with Maria Theresa Mercado (editor), Kookie Triviño (cover designer), Editha Creus (layout artist), and Monina M. Gamboa (proofreader), consultants under the Department of Communications. Staff support was also provided by Angelica Apilado and Maria Dona Aliboso. The authors would like to extend their gratitude to Andrew Jeffries and David Elzinga who provided comments, inputs, and insights from ADB operations.

Abbreviations

ABC	Anchor-Business-Consumer
AC	alternating current
ADB	Asian Development Bank
ADR	automated demand-response
ANSI	American National Standards Institute
ASEAN	Association of Southeast Asian Nations
AVR	automatic voltage regulation
BAN	body area network
BMS	building management system
BOO	build-own-operate
BOOT	build-own-operate-transfer
C&I	commercial and industrial
CAPEX	capital expenditure
CHP	combined heat and power
DC	direct current
DER	distributed energy resources
DG	distributed generator
DMC	developing member country
DNO	distribution network operator
DPR	detailed project report
DR	demand-response
DRAS	demand-response automation server
DSM	demand-side management
EIRR	economic internal rate of return
EMS	energy management system
ENPV	economic net present value
EPC	engineering, procurement, and construction
EV	electric vehicle
EVSE	EV supply equipment
FAN	field area network
FERC	Federal Energy Regulatory Commission

FIRR	financial internal rate of return
FiT	feed-in-tariff
GDP	gross domestic product
HAN	home area network
IAN	industry area network
IoT	Internet of Things
ISO	independent system operator
kV	kilovolt
kW	kilowatt
LCOE	levelized cost of electricity
MaaS	Microgrid as a Service
MCC	microgrid central controller
MMCS	microgrid monitoring and control system
MPPT	maximum power point tracker
MW	megawatt
MWD	Metropolitan Water District
NAN	neighborhood area network
NG	natural gas
NPV	net present value
NREL	National Renewable Energy Laboratory
NWS	non-wires solution
O&M	operation and maintenance
OPS	optimal power solution
P2P	peer-to-peer
PAYG	pay-as-you-go
PCC	point of common coupling
PEV	plug-in electric vehicle
PPA	power purchase agreement
PQ	power quality
PRC	People's Republic of China
PSO	particle swarm optimization
PUE	productive uses of energy
PV	photovoltaic
QTP	qualified third party
RESCO	renewable energy service company
SHS	solar home system
SPRD	Smart Power for Rural Development
T&D	transmission and distribution
ToU	time-of-use
WAN	wide area network
US	United States

Executive Summary

This handbook serves as a guide to the applications, technologies, business models, and regulations that should be considered when evaluating the feasibility of a microgrid system to enhance power supply quality and connectivity. This handbook is meant to be a go-to guide for several key aspects of understanding microgrids—particularly on-grid microgrids for urban and industrial applications in the context of current technological pathways and power system structures in the Asian Development Bank (ADB) developing member countries (DMCs) and developed countries. Prevailing business models and emerging trends that can shape the future of this sector were also taken into consideration.

Microgrids refer to grid-connected setups of varying scale that can be islanded at will, established primarily for local reliability, resilience, and operational economics. A microgrid is a localized group of interconnected loads and distributed energy resources within clearly defined electrical boundaries (e.g., cities, communities, campuses) that act as a single controllable entity with respect to the main regional or national electric grid (macrogrid). A related setup called minigrid uses similar technology and components. Minigrids have been referred to interchangeably with microgrids partly because of their proliferation, but they are actually a distinct subset of microgrids. Minigrids are isolated, small-scale distribution networks. They are essentially a microgrid disconnected from larger electric grids, which provide power to a localized group of customers and produce electricity from small generators, often coupled with energy storage systems. Currently, majority of the world's microgrids are in the North America and the Asia and Pacific region, with most of the capacity in the Asia and Pacific region being in the People's Republic of China and Japan.

In the context of grid-connected microgrids, there are traditionally three core value propositions to the end user, although the exact combination of value drivers varies from case to case—access to electricity (social), fuel and cost savings (economic), and emission reductions (environmental). Additionally, fuel independence and uninterrupted supply and/or reliability (operational) are important value propositions too. The total value of a microgrid, hence, encompasses its power generation savings, grid services, reliability and resilience, and environmental benefits and value to the distribution grid.

Nevertheless, grid-connected microgrids have not yet achieved significant scale, mainly due to the following barriers: (i) limited number of scalable prototypes, and lack of translatable performance metrics; (ii) limited experience in scalable microgrid financing models; (iii) regulatory bottlenecks arising out of restrictions on utility franchise rights and retail market access; (iv) cybersecurity concerns and limited technical standards and interconnection protocols; and (v) technical and operational challenges such as power quality, control architecture, grid synchronization and stability, and energy management.

Microgrid projects in developing countries (including ADB DMCs) can provide gains and benefits beyond solely the energy access benefit that remote off-grid minigrids provide. A key benefit that is often overlooked by policy makers is the collateral benefit of reliability and resilience of electricity supply that grid-connected microgrids, especially commercial and industrial microgrids, can provide. This is especially important as a disaster resilience strategy in several ADB DMCs, particularly in the context of increased risk of natural disasters due to climate change.

The selection of the combination of microgrid equipment is based on the key attribute that microgrids must have the ability to maintain a balance between available supply and desirable load demand through careful marriage of supply and demand combined with intelligent control. Thus, the main components of a microgrid are (i) local generation, (ii) end-use loads and demand-side energy management, (iii) energy storage, (iv) microgrid monitoring and control system, (v) utility interconnection, and (vi) other components like power electronics and protection.

In terms of design architecture, microgrids can be classified in two ways—by their control approach, and by their power technology. Under the control approach, there can be centralized and decentralized management systems based on number of entities responsible for decision-making processes and single point of failure. Under power technology, the microgrid systems can be alternating current, direct current or hybrid systems.

From a project management perspective, the conceptualization, evaluation, design, construction, and commissioning of a microgrid follows the same broad stages as other infrastructure projects with similar stakeholders. In the case of an existing facility or brownfield microgrid, the pre-project evaluation begins with the assessment of current situation, followed by high-level assessment for both brownfield and greenfield projects. The subsequent project feasibility study should typically consider applicable policy and regulatory framework, renewable energy resource assessment, assessment of site conditions and site selection, technical viability, financial viability, and financing structure.

The business models employed for grid-connected microgrids (including technology, financing, stakeholders) to meet relevant pricing options and financing implications can be: (i) customer-owned (up-front capital investment), (ii) renewable energy service company (RESCO)-owned, (iii) utility-owned, (iv) cooperative-owned, (v) community-owned, (vi) pay-as-you-go (typically rural remote minigrids), and (vii) remote (off-grid).

The choice of business model, through which the microgrid asset is built, operated, and maintained, is an important pre-development consideration irrespective of technology choice. Business model choices are typically between up-front capital investment model and RESCO model. Within the RESCO model, variations exist, such as build-own-operate, build-own-operate-transfer, lease-to-own, and power purchase agreement models.

A financial and economic analysis of microgrids requires a study of their benefits and costs to the microgrid owner or operator, the utility or distribution network operator, and/or the end user. Microgrid value is typically shared among utilities, end users, third parties, or co-owners depending on the ownership and operating model. Financial analysis of different kinds of business models are conducted using a combination of these various methodologies—net present value, financial internal rate of return, and sensitivity analysis.

Some of the key policy and regulatory enablers for urban and/or industrial microgrids in ADB DMCs would potentially include:

(i)   specific urban and/or industrial microgrid policies at national and/or provincial levels,
(ii)   net metering or gross metering policies,
(iii)   technical standards and specifications for grid interconnection,
(iv)   open access or contestable consumer policies, and
(v)   financial risk-sharing mechanisms for debt financing.

The following four case studies of grid-connected microgrids have been featured in this handbook, primarily from a business model and economics standpoint:

(i)   Case study 1: Weymouth Water Treatment Plant in La Verne, California, United States
(ii)   Case study 2: 750 kilowatt (kW) ABB Microgrid Longmeadow Park in Johannesburg, South Africa
(iii)   Case study 3: Dawanshan Island Microgrid in the People's Republic of China
(iv)   Case study 4: 500 kW Microgrid at Nagoya Landfill, Japan.

Microgrids are poised to play a big role in the electricity ecosystem of the future with decarbonization, digitalization, decentralization (3D), and non-wires solutions being its key attributes. They could help address today's energy challenges, including an optimized way to access reliable, resilient, clean energy that can defer or replace the need for specific equipment upgrades, such as new transmission lines or transformers, by reducing the load at substation or circuit level. While there is also a case for continued addition of transmission line capacity, particularly in the context of high-level penetration of renewable energy (which are almost always intermittent) to be the backbone of our electricity system, we also need to consider that (i) good solar wind resource are often at different locations, (ii) generating electricity from renewables requires a lot of land and such land availability tends to be further away from population and load centers, and (iii) electrification of transport sector would likely require additional transmission capacity. However, as a holistic strategy, if the intent is to increase the level of renewable energy penetration in the grid, then adding transmission capacity needs to be considered in the context of, and as a complement to, grid edge investments in distribution networks and microgrids.

Microgrids also hold key relevance to the transportation sector, which as a whole consumes over 30% of primary energy. Electrifying only a small percentage of this in the coming years would translate to significant capacity. A decentralized infrastructure will allow the many actors in the electric vehicle (EV) ecosystem to capitalize on the flexibility of EVs—one promising way to do this being "vehicle-to-grid" (V2G), wherein EVs can sell demand-response (DR) services to the power grid.

Microgrids are quite relevant to the current power system situation in ADB DMCs. In general, power consuming end users in developing countries typically do not have access to high-quality reliable power and must contend with frequent power outages, in contrast to their counterparts in developed countries. Developing countries also often have weak grid infrastructure due to under-investment and poor management, leading to high power losses and theft, thereby hindering the success of business and industry. This is the value proposition of grid-connected microgrids in developing countries. Furthermore, grid-connected microgrids are the building blocks of smart grids and smart supergrids, which have the potential to help developing countries leapfrog.

The handbook briefly explores current power systems and potential drivers of microgrid deployment in these ADB DMCs: Bangladesh, India, Myanmar, Nepal, the Philippines, and Thailand. South Asia, in particular, suffers from the dual problems of second largest off-grid population in the world (next to only Sub-Saharan Africa) and relatively low quality of power supply. Approaches to promote grid-connected microgrids and replication guidance are also provided. From a policy and regulatory standpoint, governments and policy makers in ADB DMCs should aim to include microgrids (both on-grid and off-gird) in their power system planning and design. Specific policies and regulations to clarify microgrid as a distinct power asset class and their technical standards in terms of grid interconnection would go a long way in incentivizing microgrid investments. Clarity on tariffs, licensing, and permitting for microgrids would also be beneficial, while targeted concessional lines of credit and financial risk-sharing facilities from development finance institutions such as ADB would help increase access to finance for microgrids in ADB DMCs.

Smart grids are evolving because of the increased proliferation of distributed energy resources, demand-side management, energy storage, and decentralized networks such as microgrids. There is significant potential for cost, efficiency, and resource utilization improvements by enabling market-based transactions between energy producers and consumers. Some of these transactive energy arrangements can be based on peer-to-peer energy trading and blockchain technologies. Smart grid is an important application of Internet of Things, which, along with data analytics and artificial intelligence, may have benefits for microgrid capabilities and techno-commercial viability.

1 Microgrid Technologies

1.1 Overview

A microgrid is a localized group of interconnected loads[1] and distributed energy resources (DERs) within clearly defined electrical boundaries (e.g., cities, communities, campuses that act as a single controllable entity with respect to the main regional or national electric grid [macrogrid]). A microgrid can connect or disconnect from the main grid as physical and/or economic conditions dictate. It can operate on both grid-connected mode (synchronous with the grid), or on island mode (functioning autonomously and disconnected from the main electric grid).[2] A typical microgrid layout is shown in Figure 1.

Figure 1: Typical Microgrid Layout

Microgrid control system
Active management maintains balanced and stable operation

Ring bus - microgrid perimeter

Source: Microgrid Institute. www.microgridinstitute.org. All rights reserved.

---

[1]   Electricity power consumption demand of end-users.
[2]   Adapted from definitions by US Department of Energy, Lawrence Berkeley National Laboratory (LBNL), and National Renewable Energy Laboratory (NREL).

Microgrids have been described as a "novel distribution network architecture within the broader smart grids[3] concept, which is capable of more fully exploiting the full range of benefits accruing from the integration of large numbers of small-scale DERs into relatively low-voltage electricity distribution systems." (Lawrence Berkeley National Laboratory [LBNL] 2019).

A related setup called minigrid uses similar technology and components, and has often been used interchangeably with microgrids. Minigrids are isolated, small-scale distribution networks—essentially a microgrid disconnected from larger electric grids. Minigrids typically operate below 11 kilovolts (kV), have a power rating below 15 megawatts (MW), provide power to a localized group of customers, and produce electricity from small generators, often coupled with energy storage systems.[4] A larger number of such minigrids that is a distinct subset—in application and business model—of the broader microgrids often cause the two terminologies to be interchanged. Minigrids are frequently set up as a cost-effective way to electrify rural communities with low population densities, or for remote facilities where laying transmission lines to connect to the grid is difficult and expensive due to topography or distance.

Microgrids, in a more specific sense of the term, refer to grid-connected setups of varying scale that can be "islanded" at will, and established primarily for local reliability, resilience, and operational economics. Islanding is a condition in which distributed generators (DG) continue to provide power in a location even without the continued presence of electrical grid power. This handbook focuses on these islandable microgrids.

Currently, majority of the world's microgrids are in the North America and the Asia and Pacific region (Figure 2), with most of the capacity in the Asia and Pacific region coming from the People's Republic of China (PRC). While there is no central registry, a semiannual tracker[5] estimates 1,869 microgrids with total capacity of 20.7 gigawatts

Figure 2: Microgrid Capacity Share by Region, Fourth Quarter 2017

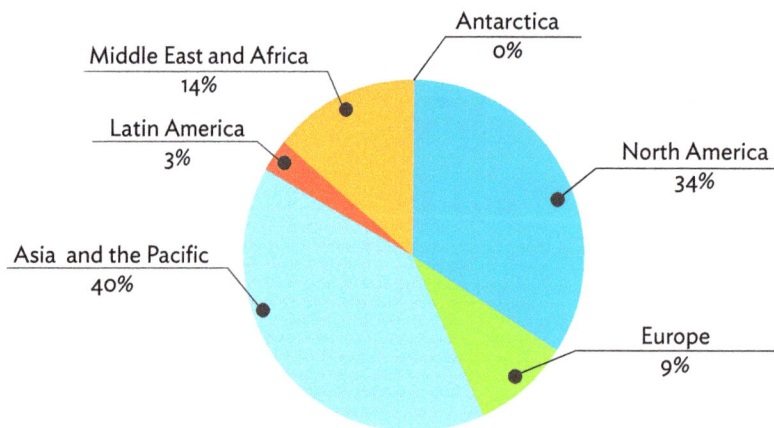

Source: F. Sioshansi. 2018. Microgrids: From niche to $100 billion market. *Energy Post*. 5 February. https://energypost.eu/microgrids-from-niche-to-mainstream/.

---

[3]   Smart grid, at the highest level, has three components: (i) improved operation of the legacy high voltage grid, e.g., through use of synchrophasers; (ii) enhanced grid-customer interaction, e.g., by smart metering or real-time pricing; and (iii) new distributed entities that were not previously common, e.g., microgrids.

[4]   Definitions from the World Bank and the United Nations Framework Convention on Climate Change (UNFCCC).

[5]   Giraldez, J. et al. 2018. Phase I Microgrid Cost Study: Data Collection and Analysis of Microgrid Costs in the United States. https://www.nrel.gov/docs/fy19osti/67821.pdf.

(GW) as of the fourth quarter of 2017. In the coming years, microgrids are expected to see a significant growth worldwide, particularly in the Asia and Pacific region and North America, with annual capacity installation and spending expected to increase approximately five times from 2018 to 2027 (Figure 3). This will require increased financing from various sources and instruments including from private and government sources.

Figure 3: Annual Microgrid Capacity and Spending, Base Scenario 2018–2027

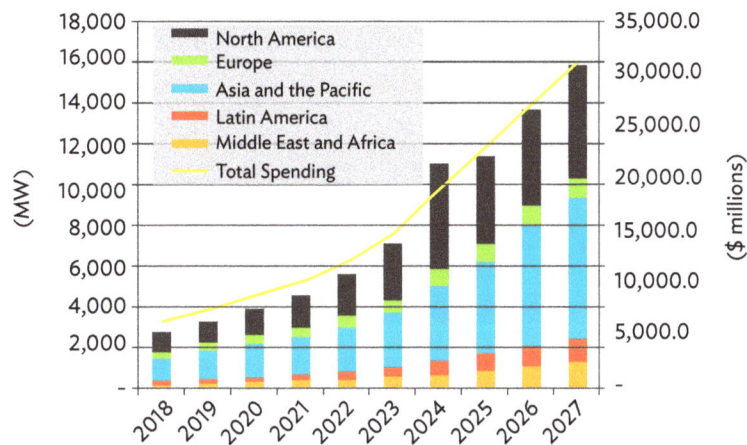

MW = megawatt.
Source: E. Wood. 2018. What's Driving Microgrids toward a $3.9B Market?. *Microgrid Knowledge*. 30 August. https://microgridknowledge.com/microgrid-market-navigant/.

1.2 Applications and Configurations

Microgrid configurations depend on their application, and have varying degrees of technological complexity and ownership structure.

Figure 4: Microgrids Classified by Technology Complexity and Ownership Structure

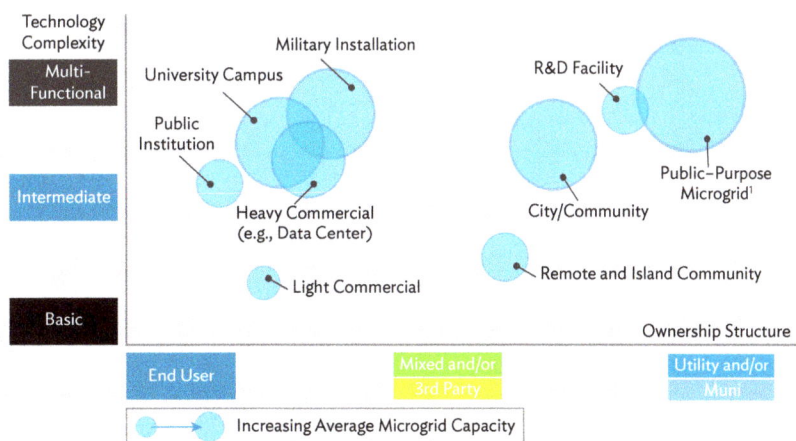

R&D = research and development.
Source: GTM Research, U.S. Microgrid Tracker, Third Quarter 2016.

The key categories in Figure 4 can be classified under five headings, which include:

(1) **Commercial and Industrial Microgrids.** These are either commercial centers or manufacturing zones with critical loads. These microgrids are often multi-owner, driven primarily by security and affordability, and are expected to grow substantially in the coming years. They are built with the goal of reducing demand and costs during normal operation. The operation of critical functions during outages is also important, especially for 24/7 high availability, high-reliability applications. One such example is the Santa Rita Jail, which houses 4,500 inmates on a 0.5 square kilometer (km^2) site. Microgrid elements were gradually added from 2004 onwards to bring it to its configuration as of 2012, driven mainly out of energy security and affordability considerations.

Figure 5: Santa Rita Jail Microgrid

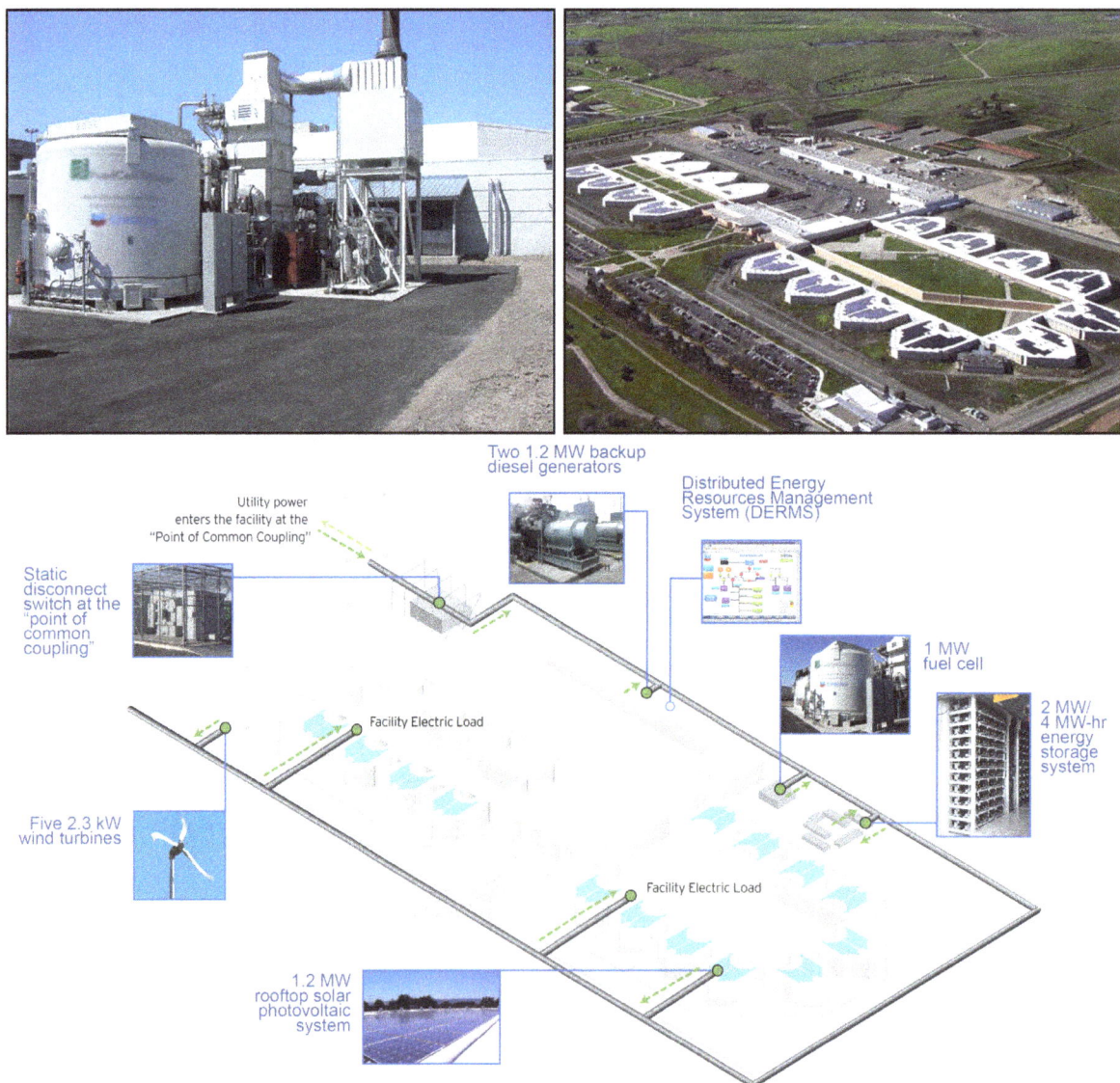

kW = kilowatt, MW = megawatt, PG&E = Pacific Gas and Electric.

Source: Scott, N. 2016. Microgrids: *A Guide to their Issues and Value. Highlands and Islands Enterprise in Partnership with the Government of Scotland.* https://www.hie.co.uk/media/5957/a-guide-to-microgrids.pdf.

(2) **Community, City, Utility Microgrids.** These are aimed toward improving the reliability for critical infrastructure, deferred asset investment, achievement of emissions and clean energy targets, and to foster community engagement. It comprises primarily residential customers and is driven mainly by the needs of affordability and security (Figure 6). However, there are impediments to their attaining widespread commercial traction until additional standards are in place and certain regulatory barriers removed.

Figure 6: Overview of Operations of a Typical Utility Microgrid

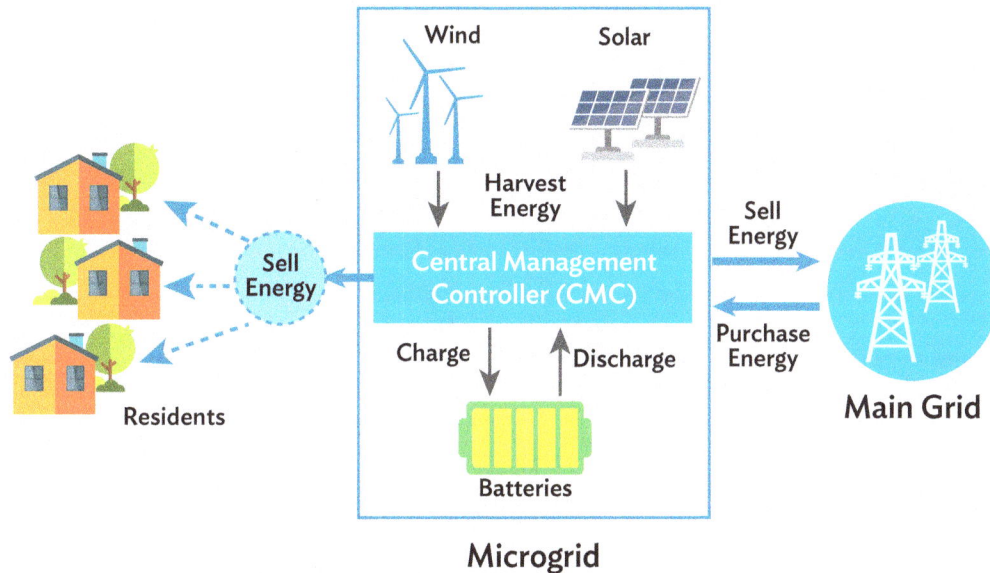

Source: Li et al. 2016. HELOS: Heterogeneous Load Scheduling for Electric Vehicle-Integrated Microgrids. *IEEE Transactions on Vehicular Technology.* PP(99). https://www. researchgate.net/publication/311502708_HELOS_Heterogeneous_Load_ Scheduling_for_Electric_ Vehicle-Integrated_Microgrids/stats.

(3) **Campus and Public Institutional Microgrids.** These have the advantage of a common ownership structure, offer good near-term development opportunity, and is a segment with the potential to develop sophisticated advanced microgrids. For instance, these microgrids accounted for 40% of the United States' pipeline of microgrids, adding 940 MW of new capacity valued at $2.76 billion by 2015 (Devi and Babu 2017). Broadly, these could target either:

(i) Research laboratories and campus housing, which comprise large heating and cooling demands with good cost reduction opportunity and potential to reduce emissions. They are usually large areas and may also double up to function as emergency shelters during extreme events such as cyclones, forest fires, and earthquakes. Combined heat and power (CHP)-based district energy solutions are often attractive in these cases because of the location's requirement of uninterrupted electrical as well as thermal service. Many campuses already have distributed generation resources and controllable loads, so microgrid technology can be overlaid to link them together to harness the additional benefit of the ability to sell excess power back to the grid (Figure 7).

(ii) Public health and safety facilities such as hospitals, police stations, fire stations, wastewater treatment plants, schools, and public transit systems, to improve reliability and lower energy consumption and cost.

Figure 7: Layout of a Typical Campus Microgrid

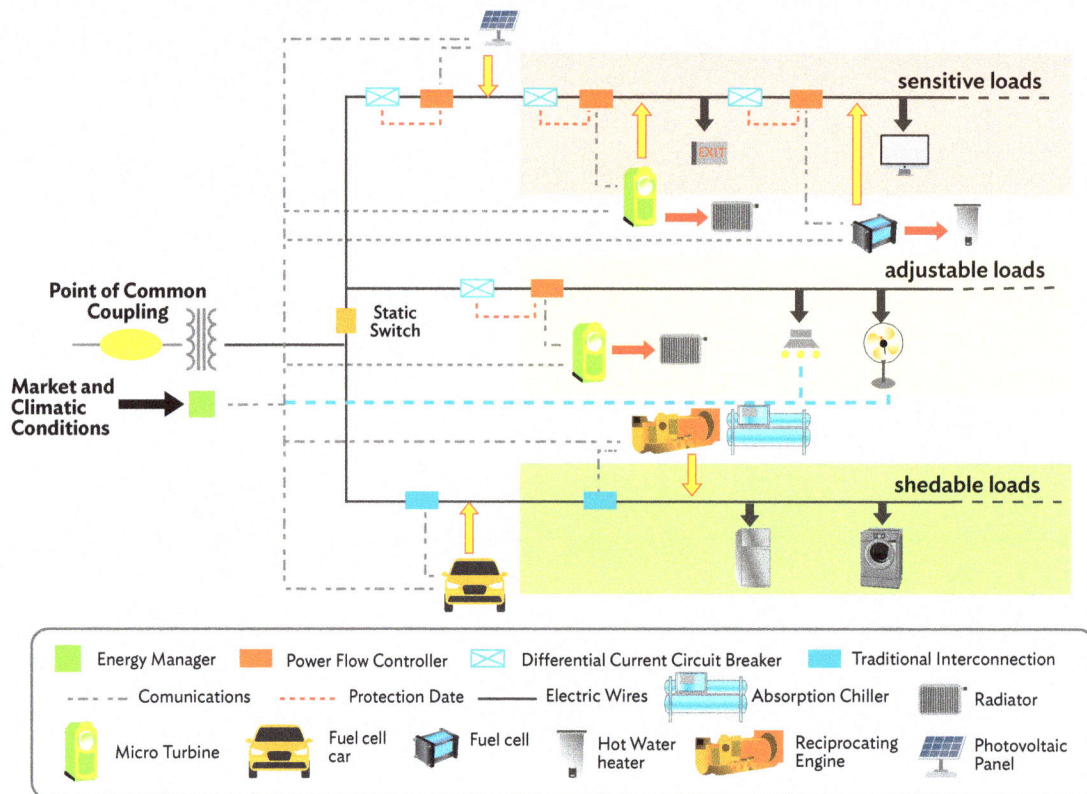

Source: Lawrence Berkeley National Laboratory (LBNL). 2019. *About Microgrids*. Microgrids at Berkeley Lab. https://building-microgrid.lbl.gov/about-microgrids-0.

(4)   **Mission-Critical Microgrids**. These are currently the smallest market segment, but are starting to pick up. These are typically seen in mission-critical applications like data centers, hospitals, laboratories, and military bases where energy security (reliability and resiliency) is the principal driver. Military microgrids focus on high reliability for mission-critical loads, strong cybersecurity and physical security requirement, "non-operationally ready" energy cost reduction, and greenhouse gas emission reduction goals at the operating bases. They make a strong case for integrating distributed renewable energy generation, so they can secure power supply without depending on the grid or any supplied fuel.

(5)   **Rural and Remote Microgrids.** This is one of the most common types of setups today. This segment accounts for the largest number of microgrids operating currently (Figure 8), but has the smallest average size. Remote microgrid communities are typically connected to the rural distribution system in weak grid areas where it is prohibitive to bring in new transmission lines for backup due to distance, cost, or physical barriers, such as in mountainous or remote communities. The main benefits of these microgrids include reliable energy supply and integration of low carbon renewable energy, such as biomass, solar photovoltaic (PV), and wind power to minimize fuel dependency. Thus, pollution and energy costs are minimized. Many have existing diesel generation, and it is expected to continue to be a market segment driven by solar PV deployment, with small wind and mini and micro-hydro also projected to play a growing role. As they become larger, these remote microgrids start to experience operational constraints that can be alleviated by microgrid management and optimization techniques. Minigrids, which typically serve off-grid areas (as opposed to "weak grid" areas referred to in this category) are a subset of this.

Figure 8: Worldwide Microgrid Installed Capacity by Segment, Second Quarter, 2016

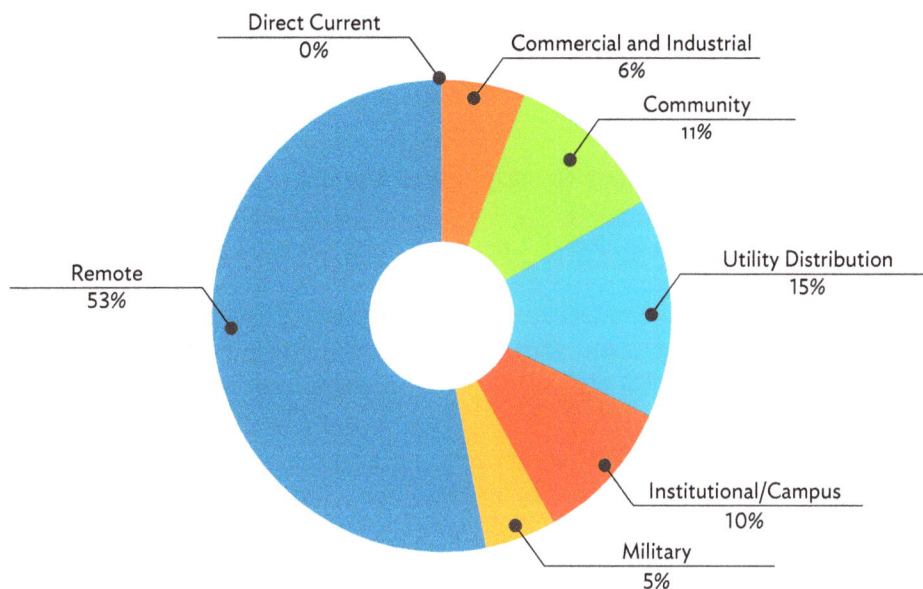

Source: Navigant Consulting. 2016; Retrieved from: https://www.amo.on.ca/AMO-PDFs/Events/16ES/PeterAsmus.aspx.

1.3 Benefits and Barriers

1.3.1 General Benefits

As mentioned in the previous section, most of the microgrids in the world today are actually minigrids for remote service, and serve consumers and loads in nonutility or non-grid connected areas, such as remote islands and communities. In these applications, the microgrid needs to provide a scaled-down version of services that the traditional electric utility would typically do. However, in terms of the fast-expanding, grid-connected segment, which is the focus of this handbook, there are traditionally three core value propositions for the end user. The exact combination of value drivers varies from case to case, but are usually a combination of the following.

Reliability. The most common objective of a microgrid, especially in the commercial and industrial (C&I) and mission-critical sectors, is to be more reliable and resilient than the utility so that the energy end user continues to have uninterrupted service even during extreme circumstances (e.g., earthquakes, storms, or power grid outages from faults on the utility grid). These "high 9" applications (referring to the level of availability ranging from 99.9% to 99.999%) are usually in hospitals, data centers, military bases, laboratories, etc. In these applications that require a high 9 level of reliability, the microgrid's cost is viewed as secondary to the purpose, i.e., maintaining energy supply to the facility even under extreme conditions. In situations like these, the value of electricity is often several multiples of its actual cost.

Cost savings. Another objective for microgrids is to supply cheaper power than that from the utility. In this case, the microgrid produces and manages an energy supply with its internal generation and storage resources, to provide electricity at lesser (or at least competitive) cost compared to that which would be charged by the utility for similar service levels. A simple instance of this might be a customer-owned net metered solar PV system. However, these are usually more sophisticated, especially if installed for providing cheaper electricity than the local utility. This is because achieving lower electricity needs cost-effective generation sources, demand-side management,[6] and if possible, the trading of electricity as a "prosumer" at the microgrid point of common coupling (PCC) to the utility. A prosumer is someone who consumes and produces a product, in this case electricity. When trading electricity, the microgrid may also have other types of generation like natural gas (NG) turbines or microturbines, as well as storage, to leverage time-of-use (ToU) arbitrage opportunities that might be available with the grid.

Environmental benefits. Renewable energy is the fastest growing power source for environmental, and, increasingly, cost considerations (Lilienthal 2018). However, while this has been successful to an extent in reducing the amount of fossil fuels used, the intermittence and variability of key renewable energy sources like solar and wind limit the amount that can go into a system unless energy storage is deployed. Hence, many microgrids are now utilizing energy storage to integrate high penetrations of clean renewable power. Advanced distributed energy storage management, as well as demand-side management, potentially allows for not just the integration of higher amounts of renewable energy, but also better reliability benefit than can be achieved via centralized storage.

Figure 9: Microgrid Value Proposition Triangle

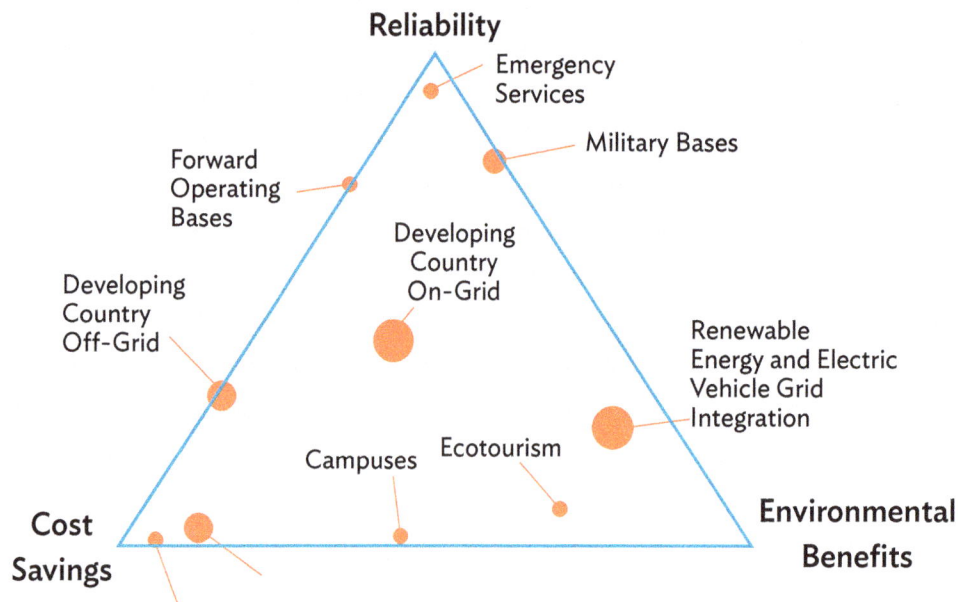

Source: Lilienthal, P. 2018. *Microgrid Value Propositions Revisited: Part One*. Homer Microgrid News. https://microgridnews. com/microgrid-value-propositions-revisited-part-one/.

Of these three core value propositions, it is the level of reliability required that usually drives the sophistication of the microgrid's design, and thereby the cost of the electricity it delivers (HDBaker 2016).

---

[6]   Ability to control loads to optimize usage of generation resources.

These three core value propositions translate into numerous potentials, can be directly and indirectly monetized, and with end-user benefits from microgrids. They

(i)   incorporate efficient, cost-competitive sources of clean energy such as CHP, solar, wind, mini-hydro, and thermal and electric storage;

(ii)   leverage thermal, kinetic, and battery storage devices to integrate variable intermittent renewable generation sources such as solar PV;

(iii)   provide the enabling infrastructure to enhance the techno-commercial viability of demand-side management (DSM) and building management systems;

(iv)   enhance resilience and reliability of electric service to end users and facilities;

(v)   function as emergency shelters in case of extreme weather, earthquakes, or fire;

(vi)   employ decentralization to reduce the concentration of risk in a few critical assets;

(vii)   develop local expertise and provide jobs;

(viii) reduce peak loads and thereby grid congestion;

(ix)   improve regional grid stability and operation;

(x)   increase the competitiveness of regional electric markets; and

(xi)   help serve the regional grid's energy, capacity, and ancillary services markets.

A well-designed regional electric grid combining large centralized power plants with distributed generation via microgrids can be built at less cost. It requires less installed generation capacity, and can operate at higher capacity factor while delivering higher reliability and resilience (Microgrid Resources Coalition [MRC] 2017).

The last few points listed above open up an evolved perspective with which microgrid users and regulators should view microgrids—not just in terms of benefits to the microgrid users, but also to the distribution grid as a whole (Figure 10).

Figure 10: Total Value of a Microgrid

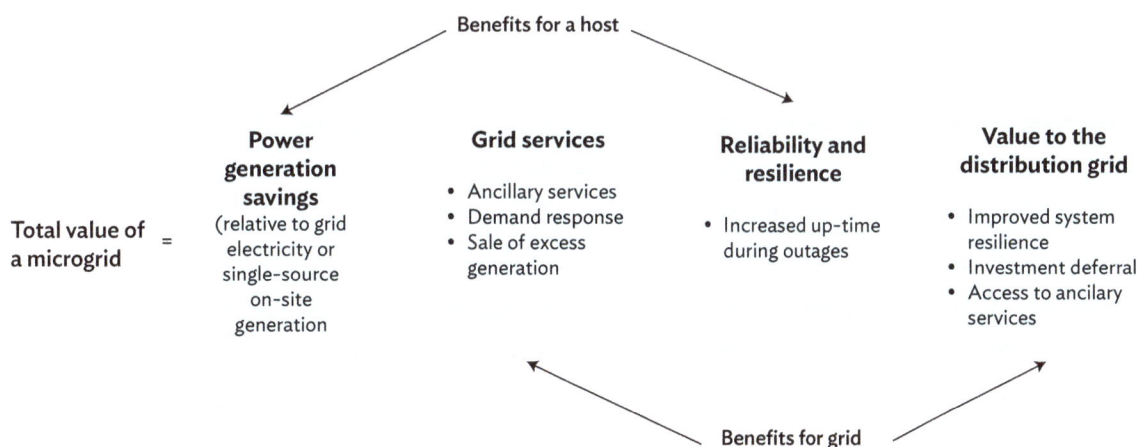

Source: Kawahara, T., ed. 2019. *Distributed Renewable Energy in Emerging Countries*. Bloomberg New Energy Finance.

1.3.2 Drivers by Application Type

The primary motivation for implementing a microgrid, while broadly defined by the microgrid benefits triangle depicted above, varies by application. The drivers for the key types are summarized in Table 1.

Table 1: Drivers by Microgrid Types

	Segments	Typical Customers	Main drivers				
			Social	Economic	Environmental	Operational	
			Access to electricity	Fuel and cost savings	Reduce CO_2 footprint	Fuel Independence	Uninterrupted supply
Off-grid	Island utilities	(Local) utility, IPP*		✓	✓	✓	(✔)
Weak grid	Remote communities	(Local) utility, IPP, Governmental development Institution, development bank	✓	✓		✓	
Grid-connected	Industrial and commercial	Mining company, IPP, oil and gas company, datacenter, hotels and resort, food and beverages		✓	(✔)	✓	✓
	Defense	Governmental defense institution		(✔)	(✔)	✓	✓
	Urban communities	(Local) utility, IPP			(✔)		✓
	Institutions and campuses	Private education institutions, IPP, Government education institution		(✔)			(✔)

IPP = independent power producer.
Source: Tam, C.W., ed. 2019. *Urban Microgrids: Enabling Utility and C&I Towards Green Digital Future.* Manila: ADB; Asia Clean Energy Forum 2019.

1.3.3 Barriers

There are currently several potential barriers to the implementation of microgrids, for which solutions are still evolving. These include:

(i)   Limited number of scalable prototype installations and all-in-one deployments

   (a)   Most deployments are customized and incrementally installed with organic increase in need. Consequently, the conceptualization and design can be time-consuming. This is compounded by the general lack of utility leadership in encouraging microgrids.

   (b)   Many microgrids are brownfield[7] to the extent that existing generation and load assets need to be integrated. While this can help reduce up-front capital costs, it may place limitations on optimal design.

(ii)   Lack of translatable microgrid performance metrics

   (a)   While installation-specific microgrid performance metrics are often documented, these may not be identical to the metrics at another installation due to customization and the uniqueness of each microgrid architecture and layout. Thus, they are not easily translatable across installations and every microgrid business case has to, in a way, reinvent the wheel, build a first principles business case (rather than rely on proven outcomes at other installations), and navigate the same early-adopter risks.

---

[7]   Brownfields are similar to greenfields except that instead of building a new asset, the private entity takes over an existing asset and usually makes an improvement to it (rehabilitation) or expands it.

(b) Consequently, the building of effective business cases, which relies on streamlined documentation of quantative and qualitative microgrid benefits, is hampered.

(iii) Limited microgrid financing models

(a) Most of the current projects are end user or utility financed, with limited access to a third party, especially private capital, mainly because microgrid projects are often not bankable from a financier's perspective. This is due to the lack of translatable performance metrics—and since fully capturing the myriad of microgrid value streams and risks—brings in additional uncertainty.

(b) To address this, stakeholders will have to develop a programmatic approach toward microgrid financing, with clearly defined benchmarks and standards that will allow potential investors to compare the relative bankability of candidate projects. Ideally, microgrids will then develop into a distinct asset class from investor perspective, and the financiers in this arena will develop standardized processes to evaluate potential investments. (Strahl, Paris, and Vogel 2015)

(iv) Restrictions from utility franchise rights and limited retail market access

(a) There is lack of regulatory familiarity as well as utility experience with microgrids. Therefore, understanding how to justify them as a grid asset can be challenging. Business case examples that clearly demonstrate value to both participants and nonparticipants from a regulatory perspective are limited. For example, there are limited instances of ability to quantify and value resilience.

(b) While in an increasing number of cases, microgrids today are producers and consumers of electricity (prosumers), in many cases they are still not fully integrated with utility generation, and sale of power to third parties utilizing the utilities' transmission and distribution (T&D) infrastructure infringes the latter's franchise rights. Regulations that allow this will enhance the financial viability of microgrids.

(v) Cybersecurity concerns

Security-sensitive applications in grid-connected operation are vulnerable in the absence of cyber secure standards, architectures, and devices. Common points of vulnerability are wired and wireless communications networks used to control, monitor, repair, and reboot processes of the system or equipment within it. For example, the communications ports in smart home controllers, common in microgrids, are a weak link. While utility scale grid management systems routinely scan for malicious elements trying to hack into the macrogrid, microgrid control systems need to achieve a similar standard of security on smaller budget with fewer equipment, sensors, and less analytics.

(vi) Limited standards and interconnection protocols

Given the large variety of processes in a microgrid, several standards are applicable to microgrids for different purposes (Figure 11 presents a pictorial overview, and additional detail is listed in Appendix 4). However, many microgrid function specifics are still not comprehensively covered in these and enhancements continue to be made.

(vii) Technical and operational challenges

(a) These include power quality (e.g., harmonics management, voltage and/or frequency control); grid synchronization; control strategies; control architecture; energy management; energy optimization; stability; protection protocols (e.g., during grid synchronization, transitions from islanded to grid-connected operation modes); initial design process of the microgrid; and the additional skill sets required of the operators.

(b) Table 2 includes a list of the key microgrid technical and operational challenges, and ways to address them.

Figure 11: Key Standards Used in Microgrids

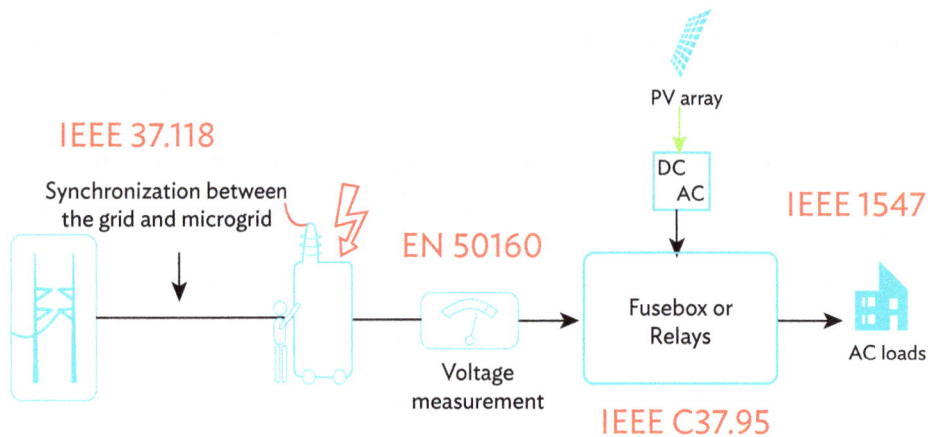

AC = alternating current, DC = direct current, EN =European Engineering Standard, IEEE =Institute of Electrical and Electronics Engineers, PV = photovoltaic.

Source: Elizondo, L.R., ed. 2018. *Solar Energy: Integration of Photovoltaic Systems in Microgrids.* Delft: Delft University of Technology (TU Delft). https://ocw.tudelft.nl/courses/solar-energy-integration-photovoltaic-systems-microgrids/.

Table 2: Microgrid Technical and Operational Challenges

Microgrid Challenges	Methods and Technologies	Comments and Examples
Power quality. Power quality disturbances in AC microgrids adversely affect system frequency and voltage via voltage fluctuations, voltage notching, transients, harmonic distortion, outages, and flickers. Sensitive end users such as hospitals, data centers, high-tech manufacturers, financial traders, research labs and communications networks, are especially affected by poor PQ. **LBNL** in 2006 estimated customer losses associated with PQ events in the United States were $79 billion a year.	Energy storage	Electrical batteries, flywheel mechanical storage, thermal storage
	Filtering	Active power conditioners (APC)
	Adequate design and proper control methods	Microgrids can be designed and controlled (frequency/active power (f-P) and voltage/reactive power (V-Q) droop controls droop control, optimal power control) active power/reactive power (PQ) that matches customer needs, including while disconnecting or "islanding" during grid power loss
	Energy storage + Filtering	Flywheel storage and active power filter
	Power electronic converters	These can be used for providing harmonic compensation, along with other control methods that can be used to keep other PQ parameters within desired limits

continued on next page

Table 2 *continued*

Microgrid Challenges	Methods and Technologies	Comments and Examples
Control strategies. Control is needed to attain required microgrid parameters such as a high PQ, clean cost-effective energy dispatch, combined heat and power management, demand-side management, supply/demand time-of-use strategies and compliance with utility grid interconnection agreements.	Primary (local control)	Frequency and/or voltage droop control
	Secondary centralized control	Non-model-based fuzzy and neutral network controllers and model-based predictive controllers
	Secondary decentralized control	Multi-agent-based control approaches
	Tertiary (optimization) control	Part of the main utility grid and not microgrid itself
Microgrid control architecture. Suitable selection and configuration of control architecture is a critical prerequisite for the microgrid to be able to coordinate electricity generation, storage, and demand, while considering the individual characteristics of the various microgrid components. There are two frequently employed control architectures: hierarchical approach, and multi-agent approach.	Hierarchical approach	Tasks are divided into primary, secondary, and tertiary by a master controller. The disadvantage is this has single point failure risk.
	Multi-agent approach	More complex technically. However, it is inherently resistant to single point of failure.
Energy management	Combined energy storage	Combined batteries and super capacitors, hybrid fuel cell battery
	Power generation prediction and load forecasting	Managing power flow among the different energy sources and the storage system within the microgrid
	Voltage-droop characteristic	Voltage regulation and load reactive power compensation
Energy optimization	Multi-objective programming using intelligent methods	Genetic algorithm, fuzzy neural networks, particle swarm optimization, and ant colony optimization
Stability	Proper control strategies	Supplementary control loop around the primary control loop
Protection	Adaptive protection system	
	Digital relays	
	Current limiting algorithms	
	Voltage based fault detection	
	State observer	
Modeling	Software based model	HOMER, Distributed Energy Resources (DER)-CAM (Appendix 7)
	Comprehensive small signal model	Accurate but very complex
	Reduced small signal model	Model order reduction and linearization around an operating point
	Nonlinear model	

continued on next page

Table 2 *continued*

Microgrid Challenges	Methods and Technologies	Comments and Examples
Grid synchronization. During grid disconnection and connection, system frequency and voltage control and stability need to be maintained seamlessly within acceptable limits. **Microgrids** have certain technical requirements, particularly if they incorporate several generation and load types, each with their own specific response time, control, and ramp rate. **Transitions** between grid-connected and islanded modes and voltage/voltage (v/v) also require the microgrid generation to be synchronized with the grid, ensuring safe and reliable reconnection.	Seamless grid disconnection is managed by the controlled dampening of any transients, while simultaneously using fast responding storage to counterbalance any power variations.	
	Instrumentation and control systems can be used to ensure that microgrid voltage and phase angle match the macrogrid before a live reconnection.	
	Alternatively, if the microgrid can be de-energized before reconnection, synchronization is not necessary.	

AC = alternating current, f-p / V-Q = frequency/active power and voltage/reactive power droop controls, PQ = power quality, v/v = voltage/voltage.
Sources: Sabzehgar, R. 2017. Overview of Technical Challenges, Available Technologies, and Ongoing Developments of AC/DC Microgrids. In W.P. Cao, and J. Yang, *Development and Integration of Microgrids*. doi:10.5772/ intechopen.69400.; and
Arup. 2019. *Five-Minute Guide to Microgrids*. https://www.arup.com/perspectives/publications/promotional-materials/section/five-minute-guide-to-microgrids.

1.3.4 Relevance of Grid-Connected Microgrids to Developing Countries

Microgrid projects in developing countries (including the DMCs of ADB) can, contrary to what is included in the typical conceptualization rubric, provide gains and benefits beyond the energy access advantage that remote off-grid minigrid capability provides alone. A key benefit that is often overlooked by policy makers is the collateral benefit of reliability and resilience of electricity supply that grid-connected microgrids, especially C&I microgrids, can provide. This oversight by policy makers is mainly because of the huge low-hanging opportunity for remote minigrids to expand energy access and improve social conditions. However, a reliable and stable power supply is an accompanying benefit that can also be valuable for C&I customers in the weak grid areas that are commonly encountered in developing countries. For instance, power outages are estimated to cost African countries 1%–2% of their gross domestic product (GDP), with Tanzania at a whopping 15% of its GDP. In Latin America, India, and several countries of the Association of Southeast Asian Nations (ASEAN), weak unreliable grids affect C&I companies. This results in excessive rental premiums on enclaves with reliable backup, usually provided via diesel generators. The 2015 worldwide sales of these diesel generators was 25 MW, and for which there is large opportunity to be replaced with renewable energy microgrids (World Business Council for Sustainable Development [WBCSD] 2017). Figure 12 shows two cases that illustrate this.

Figure 12: Developing Country Commercial and Industrial Microgrid Value Creation

Source: World Business Council for Sustainable Development (WBCSD). 2017. *Microgrids for Commercial and Industrial Companies: Delivering Increased Power Reliability, Lower Energy Cost and Lower Emissions.* https://docs.wbcsd.org/2017/11/WBCSD_microgrid_INTERACTIVE.pdf.

Given the importance of this segment that sometimes gets neglected in microgrid projects in developing countries, two additional examples below underscore the importance of the reliability provided by even basic grid-connected C&I setups in both rural and urban areas of developing countries (WBCSD 2017):

(i)   In Saint Damien Hospital, a hospital in Haiti, 650 kilowatts (kW) of rooftop solar and a 650 kW diesel generator with 500 kW Li-ion battery are capable of providing the entire energy requirement (the diesel generator being relatively large due to roof top size limitation).

(ii) At SNIM iron ore mine in Mauritania, 4.4 MW of wind and 16 MW of diesel generation supplement the often-inadequate grid supply to avoid costly equipment stoppages.

This criticality of this aspect is further justified with specific reference to ADB DMCs in Section 3.

1.4 Components of a Microgrid

Five broad categories of components are needed to build a functioning grid-connected microgrid: local generation, energy storage, end-use loads, utility interconnection, and a microgrid control system (Figure 13).

Figure 13: Microgrid Schematic Showing Five Broad Categories of Components

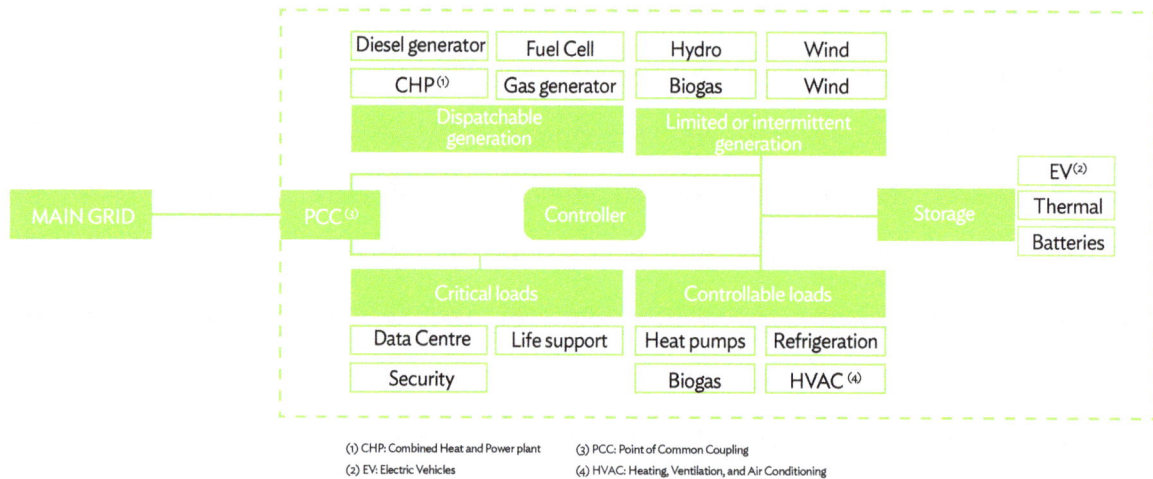

| Diesel generator | Fuel Cell | Hydro | Wind |
| CHP(1) | Gas generator | Biogas | Wind |

Dispatchable generation | Limited or intermittent generation

MAIN GRID — PCC(3) — Controller — Storage — EV(2) / Thermal / Batteries

Critical loads	Controllable loads
Data Centre	Life support	Heat pumps	Refrigeration
Security		Biogas	HVAC(4)

(1) CHP: Combined Heat and Power plant   (3) PCC: Point of Common Coupling
(2) EV: Electric Vehicles   (4) HVAC: Heating, Ventilation, and Air Conditioning

Source: World Business Council for Sustainable Development (WBCSD). 2017. *Microgrids for Commercial and Industrial Companies.* https://www.wbcsd.org/Programs/Climate-and-Energy/Energy/REscale/Resources/Microgrids-for-commercial-and-industrial-companies.

The selection of the combination of microgrid equipment is based on the key attribute that microgrids must carefully manage supply and demand with intelligent control of any imbalance. The considerations, as seen in Section 1.3, are reliability, sustainability, and affordability, along with the local grid characteristics and availability.

1.4.1 Local Generation

A microgrid must be able to supply energy to its connected loads independent of the utility, so generation sources must exist within the microgrid. These sources could range from readily controlled to intermittent, to not controllable. This could be renewable (e.g., solar PV, wind, biomass; or less frequently used such as solar thermal, hydro, micro-hydro, tidal) or nonrenewable (e.g., diesel, NG, combustion turbines, reciprocating engines, cogeneration, CHP, turbines, microturbines).

The selection of energy source needs to be adjusted to the demands on the microgrid, such as the desired generating capacity, required firmness level,[8] ramp rate, renewable energy targets, and availability of fuel (and fuel storage requirements). Brownfield microgrid setups often start with some form of existing generation already onsite, such as existing diesel generators, solar panels, or cogeneration facilities. The existing generation resources influence the additional distributed generation capacity required to be added for supporting the microgrid. Recent decreases in the price solar PV modules and other forms of renewable energy such as wind and biomass, along with energy storage, have enhanced the economic feasibility and attractiveness of renewable energy-based microgrids.

---

[8] Ability of the generator need to start at any time to produce energy.

Economies of scale apply across almost all the generating technologies, implying that smaller generators have a higher unit cost of installation cost compared to larger ones, and consequently a higher repetition of cost of energy for generation. For example, a 5 kW residential rooftop solar PV system might cost about $4 per watt to install, whereas a 50 MW utility scale solar PV farm could cost $2 per watt installed (HDBaker, 2016). Additionally, costs decline with increase in technology maturity. For example, solar PV panel costs are steadily declining. Furthermore, there are technology-specific considerations. Solar-based remote microgrids have some inherent challenges such as maintenance of the modules, since performances decrease significantly when temperature rises or it gets coated with dust or is exposed to high moisture, as well as the energy storage requirements for intermittent generation sources such as solar or wind. Intermittence is a particularly relevant aspect in economic considerations, since energy storage systems often comprise a significant fraction of the total microgrid cost, and larger intermittent capacity necessitates more storage capacity. This is one of the reasons microgrids often include quick ramping yet relatively cheap natural gas as part of a power source. Common microgrid generation sources are listed in Table 3. Additional details of renewable and nonrenewable distributed generation sources are in Appendixes 1 and 2.

Table 3: Characteristics of Common Microgrid Generation Sources

Characteristics	Solar	Wind	Micro-Hydro	Diesel	CHP
Availability	Dependent on geographical location	Dependent on geographical location	Dependent on geographical location	Anytime	Dependent on source
Output Power	DC	AC	AC	AC	AC
Control	Uncontrollable	Uncontrollable	Uncontrollable	Controllable	Dependent on source
Typical interface	Power electronic converter (DC-DC-AC)	Power electronic converter (AC-DC-AC)	Synchronous of induction generator	None	Synchronous generator
Power flow control	Maximum Power Point Tracker and DC link voltage control	MPPT, pitch and link voltage control	Controllable	Controllable	Automatic Voltage Regulation and governor

AC = alternating current, CHP = combined heat and power, DC = direct current, MPPT = maximum power point tracker.
Source: ADB.

1.4.2 End-Use Loads and Demand-Side Energy Management

The type of end-use devices determines the electrical loads that the microgrid has to be capable of handling, which in turn influences the power-generating capacity and storage requirements. For instance, cellphone charging imposes minimal capacity requirement on the system, but connecting an airconditioner to a solar PV-based microgrid can cause challenges in managing electric loads because of its large continuous power consumption. In reality, a microgrid does not consist solely of one of these extremes, but will have a range of end uses to be served.

Microgrid energy loads range in controllability characteristics from critical loads like data centers or hospital life support equipment at one end of the spectrum, to adjustable controllable loads like air conditioning, lighting, or grid dispatch at the other end. This latter category of loads can be temporarily curtailed or adjusted in line with flexible user requirements, and most modern microgrids will have the capability to control these end uses to optimize the utilization of generation and storage resources.

Each type of supply (local generation), demand (end-use loads) and storage can be categorized on the basis of their controllability, dependability, and criticality (Figure 14).

Figure 14: Characteristics of End-Use Loads and Generation

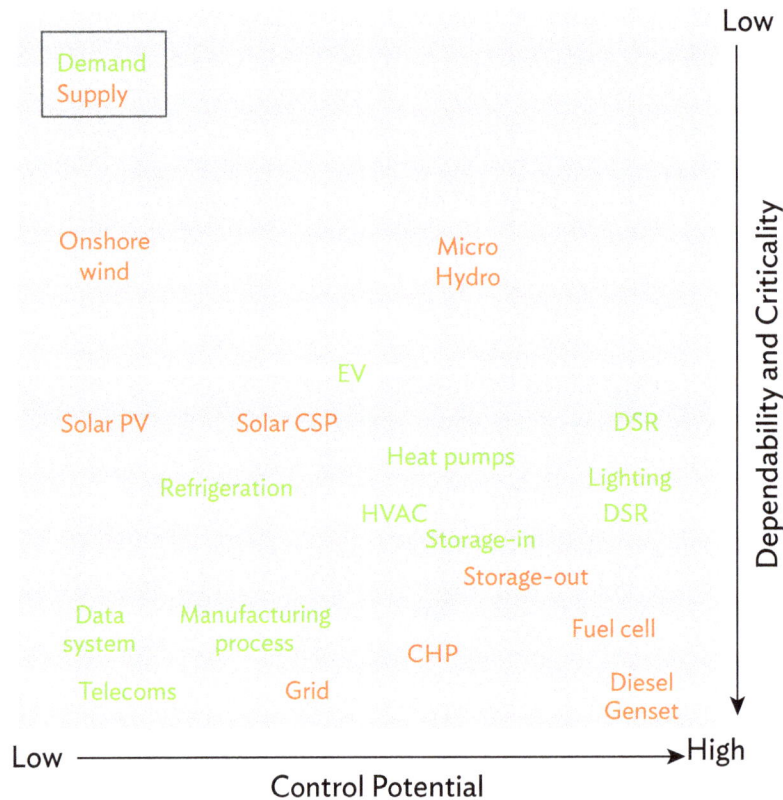

CHP = combined heat and power, CSP = concentrated solar power, DSR = demand-side response, EV = electric vehicle, HVAC = heating, ventilation, and air conditioning

Source: Arup. 2019. *Five-Minute Guide to Microgrids*. https://www.arup.com/perspectives/publications/promotional-materials/section/five-minute-guide-to-microgrids.

Demand-response (DR) is defined by Federal Energy Regulatory Commission as "changes in electric usage by end-use customers from their normal consumption patterns in response to changes in the price of electricity over time, or incentive payments designed to induce lower electricity use at times of high wholesale market prices or when system reliability is jeopardized." DR is a subset of DSM, which includes immediate real-time measures as well as long-term and permanent energy efficiency measures. OpenADR is a standard that supports a range of automated demand-response signals from the utility's demand-response automation server (DRAS) to automatically control connected equipment in the end-user premises (Figure 15).

Figure 15: System Architecture of a Typical Automated Demand-Response Implementation

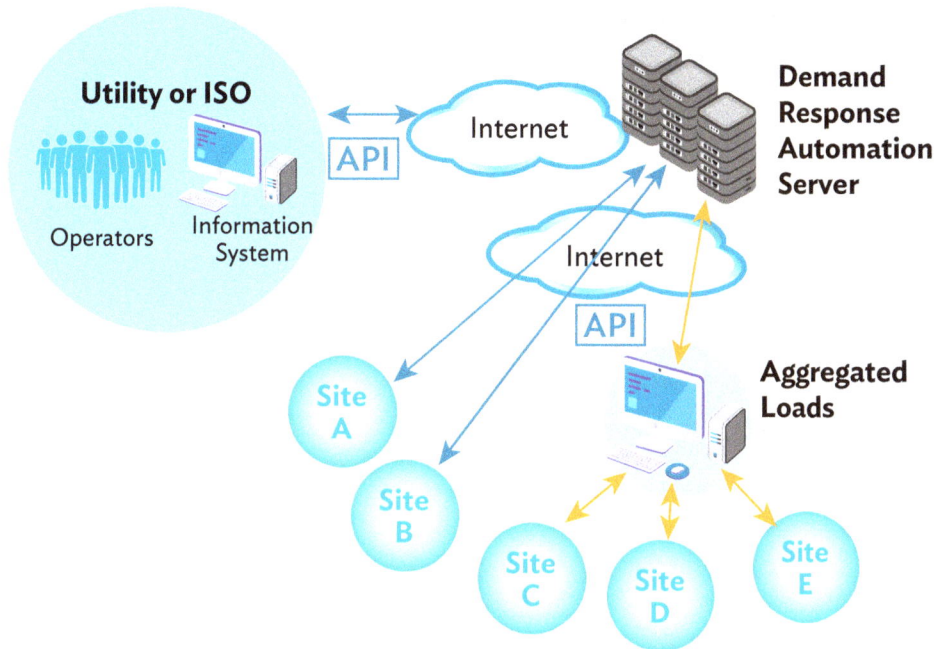

API = application programming interface, ISO = independent system operator.

Note: The demand-response automation server (DRAS) sends price and other commands to individual loads or aggregated loads (including those within microgrids).

Source: Lawrence Berkeley National Laboratory as cited by Samad, T., E. Koch, and S. Petr. 2016. *Automated Demand Response for Smart Buildings and Microgrids: The State of the Practice and Research Challenges. Proceedings of the IEEE.* 104(4). pp. 726–744. doi:10.1109/ JPROC.2016.2520639.

Microgrids open new possibilities in the realm of DR as the control actions need not be limited to controllable flexible loads, but can extend to dispatchable onsite generators and storage, all of which can be harnessed in an integrated manner by the microgrid monitoring and control system (MMCS). This would allow for noncritical loads to be shut off or turned down, dispatachable generation to be activated, and storage to be harnessed, all concurrently, which would in turn allow for enhanced participation in DR programs or arbitrage opportunities that may exist in regional power markets or service jurisdictions where ToU rates are available. Thus, microgrids potentially present conducive conditions for advanced, price incentivized, unified responses to be leveraged across a wider range of assets, by way of DSM and DR schemes. (Samad, Koch, and Petr, 2016). Figure 16 shows one such implementation at Los Angeles Air Force Base. Although there are no distributed energy resources (DER) in this case, they seek to use the charge capacity in the batteries of plug-in electric vehicles while connected to the EV supply equipment, for providing ancillary services such as frequency regulation, to the grid, with DER-CAM optimizer software to determine the optimal charging schedule functioning as the de facto energy management system (EMS).

Figure 16: System Architecture of a Microgrid that Uses Automated Demand-Response

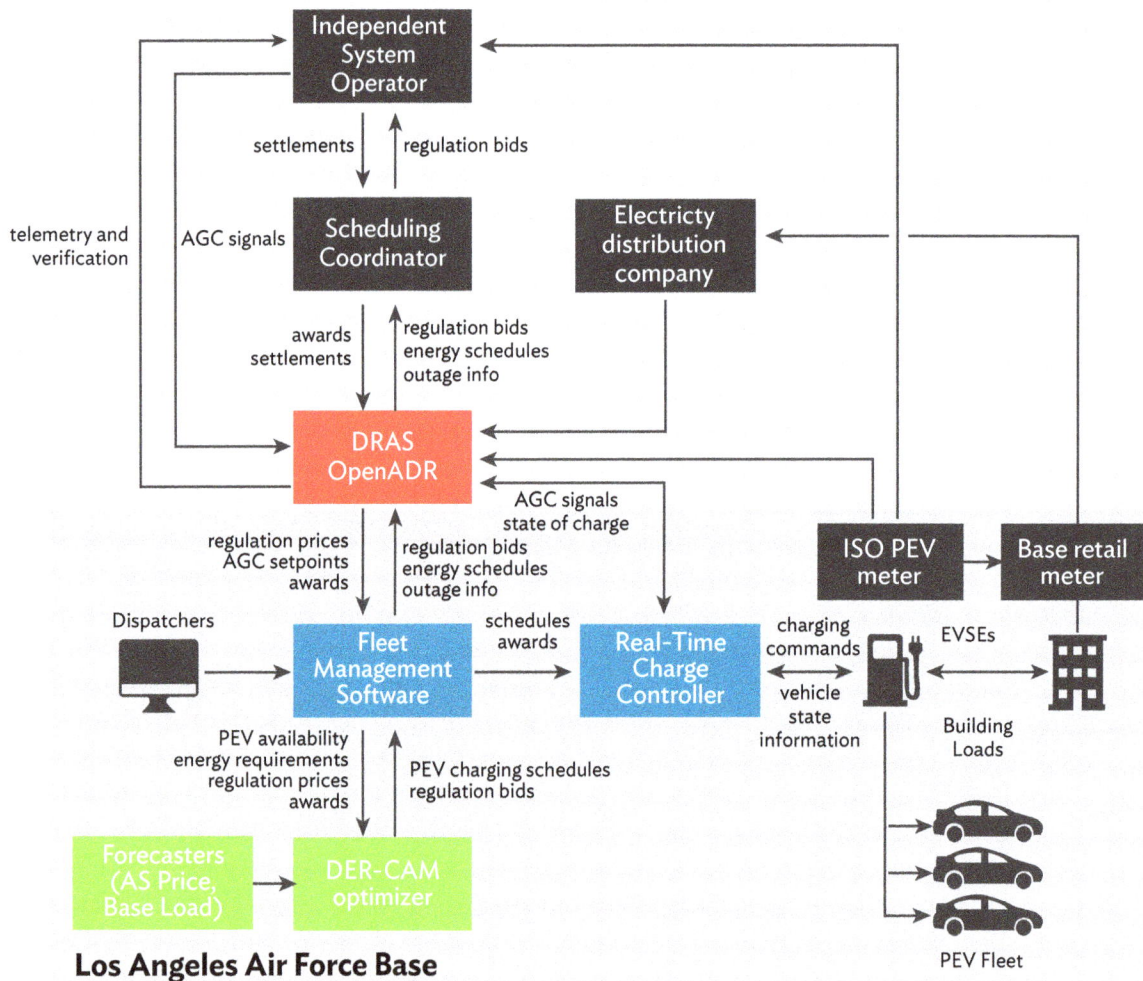

Los Angeles Air Force Base

AGC = automatic gain control, DER-CAM = distributed energy resources customer adoption model, EVSEs = electric vehicle supply equipment, ISO = independent system operator, PEV = plug-in electric vehicle.

Source: Samad, T., et. al. 2016. *Automated Demand Response for Smart Buildings and Microgrids: The State of the Practice and Research Challenges.* Proceedings of the Institute of Electrical and Electronics Engineers. 104(4). pp. 726–744. doi:10.1109/JPROC.2016.2520639.

From another perspective, DR can also be used internally within the microgrid to incentivize "rational" flexible end-use equipment to preferentially consume when cheaper sources of internal generation are available, thus minimizing import of electricity from the utility grid. In a microgrid, demand-response can potentially be executed at a more granular level than the typical regional grid or independent system operator (ISO) level, via the MMCS, with the MMCS then doubling up as the DRAS to control the facilities in the microgrid via an EMS, BMS, or individually controlled end-use devices. This scenario has the added advantage that microgrids (especially C&I or campus microgrids) contain these controllable production, storage, and consumption sources within a "walled" environment, implying simpler control and fewer cybersecurity concerns.

1.4.3 Storage

Microgrids must have some form energy storage as a means to time-shift own generation to match load demands, as well as a critical fallback supply in islanded mode operation. With energy storage, the microgrid can absorb and store the energy generated at times when supply exceeds demand, and to subsequently return it at times when demand exceeds supply (e.g., evening peaks once solar PV generation is not available). While there are some inefficiencies from storage and line losses, these are minimal compared to the value that storage can deliver. Energy storage can also be leveraged for arbitrage in wholesale power markets or with time-based rates such as real-time, peak, and ToU pricing.

The energy storage technology is chosen based on the size of the microgrid and reaction time required. For instance, for remote microgrids or smaller grid-connected microgrids, batteries are the most commonly used storage technology because the storage capacity required by the microgrid does not justify the higher costs associated with other storage technologies. Batteries can also be used to provide the ancillary services required within a microgrid. Large-scale storage technologies, such hydro-based storage or thermal storage, while cheaper for time shifting operations, have high initial costs that make their implementation in smaller and microgrids challenging.

Figure 17 provides a summary of various storage technologies in relation to their role in microgrids. It includes a comparison of energy storage sources in the range of 1–10 MW, which are typically found in microgrids. More details on the various energy storage technologies can be found in ADB's 2018 handbook on the topic of energy storage.[9]

Figure 17: Comparison of Energy Storage Sources Used in Microgrids

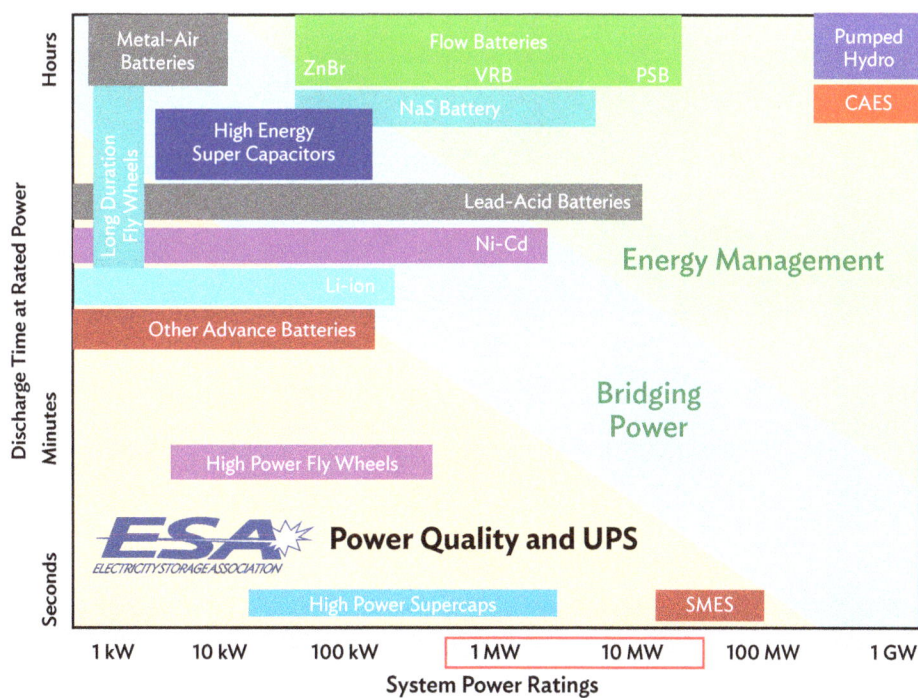

CAES = compressed air energy storage, GW = gigawatt, MW = megawatts, SMES = superconducting magnetic energy storage.
Source: Howitt, Mark. 2018. Gigawatt Scale Storage for Gigawatt Scale Renewables. *Journal of Energy and Power Engineering*, Vol. 12. https://www.researchgate.net/publication/325622672_Gigawatt_Scale_Storage_for_Gigawatt_Scale_Renewables.

---

[9]   ADB. 2018. *Handbook on Battery Energy Storage System*. Manila. https://www.adb.org/publications/battery-energy-storage-system-handbook.

1.4.4 Microgrid Monitoring and Control System

Microgrid monitoring and control systems (MMCS) tie all of the microgrid components together and maintain the real-time balance of generation and load. This control system can follow a centralized or decentralized scheme (Section 1.5). In the most basic of microgrid configurations, the control system might just be a governor controlling a diesel generator. In more complex microgrids, the MMCS comprises sensors, metering, sophisticated software platforms, and communication paths designed to allow for real-time optimization and control of the generators, energy storage, loads, and utility interface. During grid-connected operation, the MMCS needs to manage the utility interconnection and communicate with the system operations center of the utility (or independent system operator), including any DR management systems in near real time.

1.4.5 Utility Interconnection

A distinctive feature of microgrids is the interconnection with the utility's power grid, sometimes referred to as the PCC. This is what allows microgrids to operate in grid-connected or islanded modes, and transition is relatively seamlessly between both. If there is an existing utility interconnection, it lays the foundation for what additional hardware may be needed for the microgrid. This includes elements ranging from existing relays and meters in the substation and distribution equipment, to switchgears and power converters in the microgrid (Planas et al. 2015).

During grid-connected operation, the microgrid-utility interconnection at the PCC must be designed to allow for safe and reliable parallel and concurrent operation of the microgrid and the utility macrogrid. The existing utility equipment may need to be upgraded to handle the various changes that occur when islanding a microgrid. For reliability and resilience, focused microgrids where relatively frequent islanded mode operation is anticipated; the PCC must also incorporate equipment to allow for seamless disconnection and reconnection of the microgrid to the power grid. This re-synchronization of the two systems is a complex process and failure to adequately design for this function can result in instability of both the microgrid and the main power grid. Accordingly, islanding of microgrids must be addressed at both technical and policy levels (safety concerns, potential end user equipment damage, reclosing scenarios, inverter prioritization).

1.4.6 Other Components

Power Electronics

Power electronics interfaces are used to connect and manage the various components within a microgrid, e.g., generators to loads to storage. Different conversion steps such as direct current (DC)–alternating current (AC), AC–DC or DC–DC may be needed to match the input and output voltages of a single component to a microgrid voltage.

Figure 18: Power Electronics Interfaces in a Microgrid

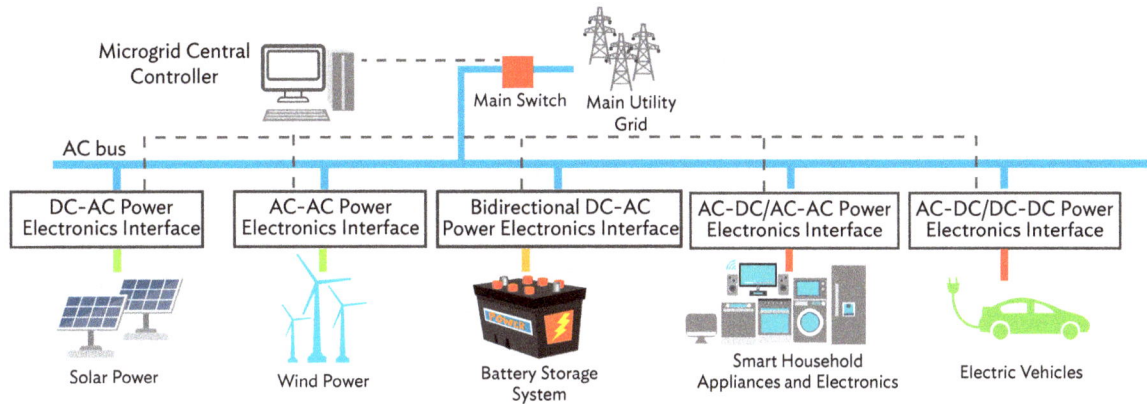

AC = alternating current, DC = direct current.
Source: Sabzehgar, R. 2017. Overview of Technical Challenges, Available Technologies, and Ongoing Developments of AC/DC Microgrids. In W.P. Cao, and J. Yang, *Development and Integration of Microgrids*. doi:10.5772/ intechopen.69400.

Protection

Protection is an important element in the design of microgrids. It is needed for the microgrid as a whole, as well as for cycle-level controls. It must act almost instantly and be carefully programmed to differentiate between grid-connected and islanded operating modes. In a grid–tied mode of operation, the protection is simplified by the potentially large fault currents, whereas these fault currents may have relatively low values in islanded mode due to integrated power electronics interfaces in microgrid. This low current capacity in islanded mode is not sufficient to trip conventional overcurrent protection. Therefore, an adaptive protection system is needed to change relay settings in real time to guarantee that the microgrid is always protected. Another solution could be utilizing digital relays equipped with a communication network to protect the microgrid. An easier way to address the protection issue is to design the microgrid to, in a fault situation, enter islanded mode before any protection action takes place.

Monitoring

There are many parameters in a microgrid such as voltage, frequency, and power quality that must be continuously monitored. Several monitoring schemes have been proposed, and several vendors supply monitoring components and solutions. Monitoring is simpler in DC microgrids than in AC microgrids. Fewer variables need to be monitored and controlled, as frequency and reactive power issues do not exist (Planas et al. 2015).

Power Converters

DERs and loads are generally connected to the distribution lines of the microgrid through power converters. They adapt the current and voltage levels of the microgrid to the connected units. Power converters vary by microgrid parameters and type, but in general, power conversion efficiency is higher in DC systems than AC systems, and mainly depends on the technology of the primary source and AC/DC load ratios (Planas et al. 2015).

Communication

Robust communication pathways are essential in microgrid implementation to ensure stable, reliable, and optimal operation, since the presence of distributed generation and loads and interaction between all the nodes within a microgrid substantially increases the complexity of power system operation and control, and thereby, communications. The microgrid communication network needs to guarantee a high level of reliability, with bidirectional and interoperable connectivity among the microgrid resources. In a way a microgrid's communication network can be considered a bridge between its physical infrastructure, and its control and protection processes. This contrasts with the traditional power grid structure, which typically lacks the aforementioned connectivity, as it is meant to function as a centralized unidirectional system. Systems architecture, standards, and tools are involved in designing how a microgrid will communicate internally using one or more languages or protocols, through wired (fiber, copper) or wireless (radio, cellular) communication pathways, some of which may already be existing.

Grid-connected microgrids are rarely stand-alone, but interact and communicate with the traditional electric grid on one side and industrial, commercial, institutional, residential, and other end uses on the other, which may contain sub-grids (Figure 19). Microgrids and these networks they interact with are broadly classified as wide area networks, industry area networks, field area networks, neighborhood area networks, body area networks, and home area networks. The communications technologies and standards used in these applications are shown in Figure 20.

Figure 19: High-Level Topology of Microgrids and their Interacting Networks

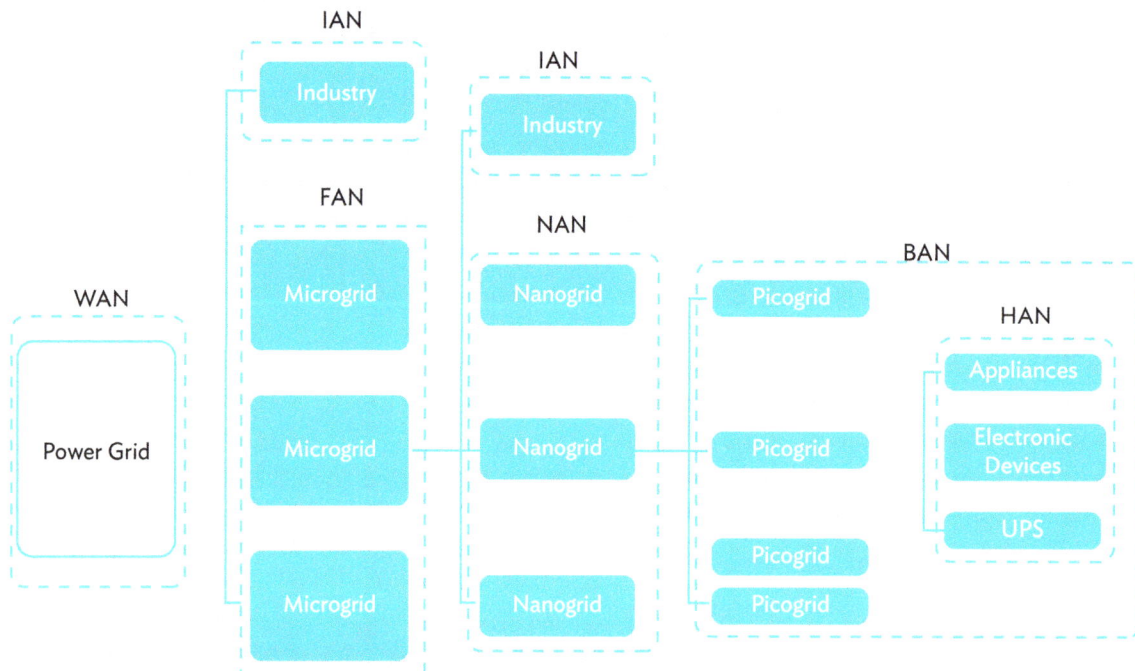

BAN = body area network, FAN = field area network, HAN = home area network, IAN = internet area network, NAN = near-me area network, UPS = uninterruptible power supply, WAN = wide area network.

Source: Elizondo, L.R., ed. 2018. *Solar Energy: Integration of Photovoltaic Systems in Microgrids*. Delft: Delft University of Technology (TU Delft). https://ocw.tudelft.nl/courses/solar-energy-integration-photovoltaic-systems-microgrids/.

Figure 20: Microgrid Communication Technologies and Standards

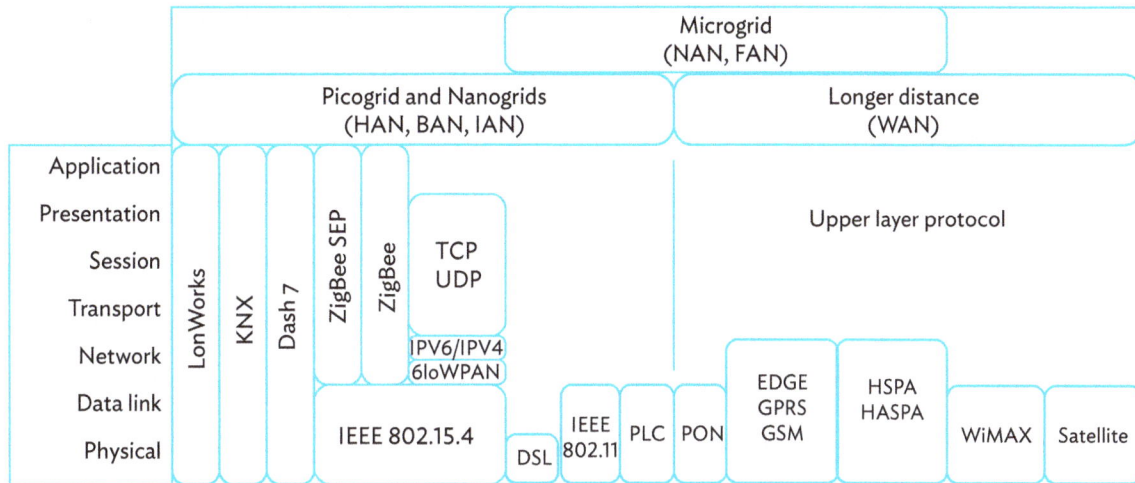

BAN = building area network, DSL = digital subscriber line, FAN = factory area network, GPRS = general packet radio service, GSM = global system for mobile communications, HAN = home area network, HASPA = high speed packet access, HSPA = high speed packet access, IAN = industrial area network, IEEE = Institute of Electrical and Electronics Engineers, NAN = neighborhood area network, PLC = power line communications, PON = passive optical network, TCP = transmission control protocol, UDP = user datagram protocol, WAN = wide area network, WiMAX = worldwide interoperability for microwave access.

Source: Elizondo, L.R., ed. 2018. *Solar Energy: Integration of Photovoltaic Systems in Microgrids*. Delft: Delft University of Technology (TU Delft). https://ocw.tudelft.nl/courses/solar-energy-integration-photovoltaic-systems-microgrids/.

Cybersecurity

Finally, some form of cybersecurity is essential. Given the extensive communication and controls, there is vulnerability to cybersecurity threats wherein a single infected computer can spread a virus on to the network, thereby affecting an entire microgrid. Microgrid operators and individual smart home owners usually rely on their equipment providers to design a cybersecure microgrid. A global safety consulting and certification company[10] published in July 2017, the first edition of a cybersecurity standard.[11] This was subsequently also published as an American National Standards Institute (ANSI) standard. Adoption of this standard by equipment providers will help improve cybersecurity in microgrids. (CleanTechnica 2018)

Components that are more robust, versatile, and durable incur greater up-front costs. However, higher microgrid capital costs can often be justified if the negative repercussions of a customer outage are large (e.g., financial firm data center outage, air traffic control outage, life support system outage, spoiled batch in a semiconductor fabrication process). Accordingly, while the enhanced reliability and resilience provided by more sophisticated microgrids might cost more, it provides value that is often multiples of the additional cost. Therefore, the customer's objective should drive the microgrid's design.

---

10   UL. https://www.ul.com/about/history.
11   UL. 2017. *UL Standard for Software Cybersecurity for Network-Connectable Products, Part 1: General Requirements, UL 2900-1.*

1.5 Microgrid Types by Design Architecture

Microgrids' design architecture can be classified in two ways: their by control approach, and by power technology.

1.5.1 Categorized by Type of Microgrid Control Approach – Centralized vs. Decentralized

One approach to classifying microgrids is based on their operational control, which is either centralized or decentralized.

In a centralized microgrid system, a single entity, the microgrid central controller (MCC) is responsible for the decision-making processes—essentially determining the setpoints of the loads, distributed generation resources, and storage units. The MCC communicates with the converters to control the active and reactive power input from the DERs and circuit breakers to control the connection of loads, DERs, and microgrid to the rest of the system (George and Chauhan 2015). Wireless communication technologies are usually used for data transmission. This architecture is a suitable option when all actors in the microgrid have common goals. As an analogy, in the traditional electric grid, centralized control is generally performed by a single entity at the transmission system operator level. Similarly, in the case of a microgrid, when applying centralized control, a single entity carries out the economic dispatch and the unit commitment calculations. The setpoints are provided to the distributed sources by an MCC (as would have been by the distribution system operator in the traditional electric grid). An MCC can be managed by the distribution system operator or by a dedicated microgrid operator, depending on the ownership structure.

Figure 21: Schematic of a Centralized Control System

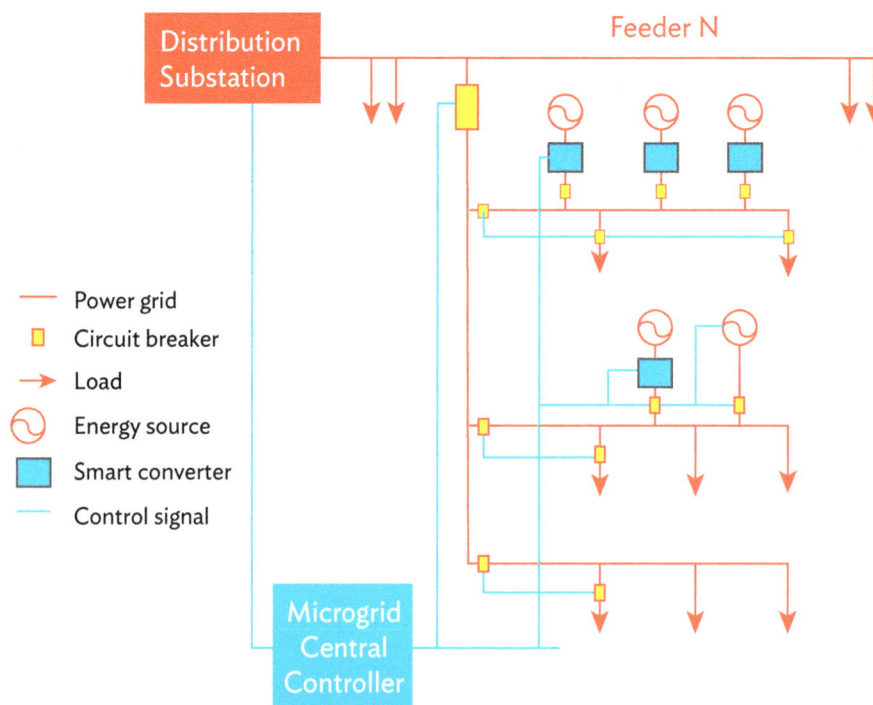

Source: George, S. and S. Chauhan. 2015. An Investigation into Centralized and Decentralized Micro-Grid Systems with Synchronization Capability and Flywheel. *International Journal of Enhanced Research in Science Technology & Engineering.* 4(5). pp. 225–248. https://pdfs.semanticscholar.org/068b/ e24d624ddfe09e4043deeac2ea72c6655499.pdf.

In a decentralized microgrid system, the internal microgrid control takes place at each controllable element in the microgrid—generators, storage, and loads. It does not require a powerful central controller and is resistant to single point of failure. Negotiation among the different actors may take place, especially because in this case, the different actors have different goals, but common aspects and calculations, like load forecasting, state estimation, and security monitoring can still be done in a centralized manner. The performance of the control algorithms depends on four key attributes:

(i)   **The number of nodes.** The DG and controllable loads that make up the microgrid affect the complexity and computational time as the number increases.

(ii) **The number of messages exchanged.** The DG and loads in microgrids are usually dispersed, and the communication systems at low voltage usually have limited bandwidth. In several cases, the number of messages required to perform a task is of primary importance. A decentralized control approach reduces the number of messages, as only a small part of the information needs to be transferred to the higher levels of the control hierarchy.

(iii) **The size and structure of the system model.** The structure and complexity of the system needs to be considered. Decisions taken by different actors might not only increase the number of nodes, but also impose extra technical and nontechnical constraints.

(iv) **The accuracy and optimality of the solution.** The convergence and accuracy of the solutions depends on the type and accuracy of the algorithms used, and the input data.

Figure 22: Schematic of a Decentralized Control System

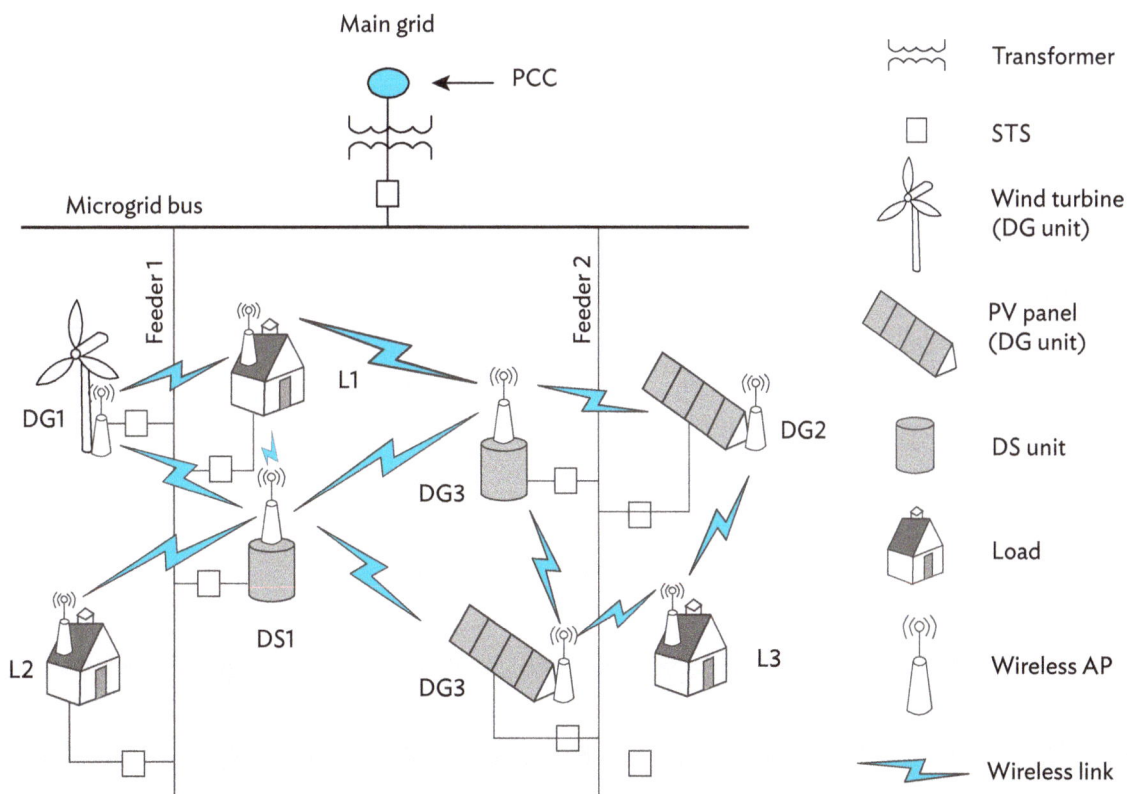

AP = access point, DG = distributed generation, DS = distributed energy storage, L = load, PCC = point of common coupling, PV = photovoltaic, STS = static transfer switch.

Source: George, S. and S. Chauhan. 2015. An Investigation into Centralized and Decentralized Micro-Grid Systems with Synchronization Capability and Flywheel. *International Journal of Enhanced Research in Science Technology & Engineering.* 4(5). pp. 225–248. https://pdfs.semanticscholar.org/068b/ e24d624ddfe09e4043deeac2ea72c6655499.pdf. .

Advantages of Centralized over Decentralized

Centralized control schemes have the following advantages:

(i)   They provide a high operation knowledge, where the main goals are clearly identified and achieved.
(ii)   They can provide global optimal solutions.
(iii) They allow an easy synchronization to the main grid, and they can effectively use real-time signals for online operation.
(iv)   Decentralized control schemes have the main disadvantage of being very complex with respect to multi-ownership and competition between the various actors or agents. Each agent seeks to achieve its own objective, such as maximizing its profits.

Figure 23: Advantages of Centralized over Decentralized Microgrids

Source: Elizondo, L.R., ed. 2018. *Solar Energy: Integration of Photovoltaic Systems in Microgrids*. Delft: Delft University of Technology (TU Delft). https://ocw.tudelft.nl/courses/solar-energy-integration-photovoltaic-systems-microgrids/.

Advantages of Decentralized over Centralized

Decentralized control schemes have important advantages:

(i)   They are suitable for fast changing infrastructures. They could easily be expanded because of their plug-and-play capabilities.
(ii)   They are reliable.

The main disadvantages of centralized control schemes are that they are computationally expensive and time-consuming. The central controller needs to run an optimization problem that takes into account a large number of distributed generation units, loads, and storage units.

The central controller has high communication requirements leading to additional costs and the risk of single point of failure.

In summary, in centralized control, the microgrid's operation is optimized by a single entity—the MCC—which assigns the setpoints to the loads, distributed generation, and storage units, toward attaining the microgrid's operating strategy and targets. In decentralized control, the decisions are taken locally by the various actors (loads, distributed generation, and storage units) and negotiations may take place, as these actors might have different goals.

Figure 24: Advantages of Decentralized over Centralized Microgrids

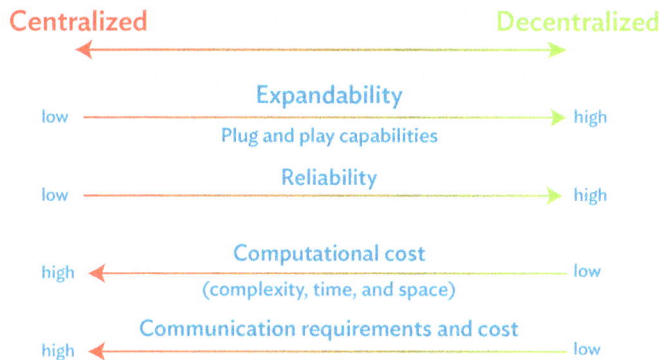

Source: Elizondo, L.R., ed. 2018. *Solar Energy: Integration of Photovoltaic Systems in Microgrids*. Delft: Delft University of Technology (TU Delft). https://ocw.tudelft.nl/courses/solar-energy-integration-photovoltaic-systems-microgrids/.

Table 4: Key Differences between Centralized and Decentralized Microgrid Control

AC = alternating current, DG = distributed generator, IC = interlinking converter, LC = load controller, MCC = microgrid central controller, PV = photovoltaic, RES = renewable energy resource.

Source: Elizondo, L.R., ed. 2018. *Solar Energy: Integration of Photovoltaic Systems in Microgrids*. Delft: Delft University of Technology (TU Delft). https://ocw.tudelft.nl/courses/solar-energy-integration-photovoltaic-systems-microgrids/.

1.5.2 Categorized by Type of Power Technology – Alternating Current vs. Direct Current vs. Hybrid

Microgrids can also be classified based on the type of power distribution technology used, AC, DC, or hybrid. While several considerations go into the eventual selection of a power technology for the microgrid, the most suitable option is likely to be an AC microgrid because it needs minimal modifications on the existing installations. However, DC or hybrid microgrids often have better performance and should be considered for new installation greenfield microgrids. As of existing installations, AC microgrid technologies dominate when it comes to integration of local power generation and consumption for both on-grid and off-grid applications, but as DC microgrid technologies develop further, there is likely to be greater adoption as well combinations of the two approaches, or hybrid configurations.

AC microgrid. In an AC microgrid, all the DER (renewable and nonrenewable), energy storage devices and end-use loads (both AC and DC) are connected to a common AC bus (backbone network). When the microgrid's energy generation exceeds all the loads on it, the microgrid can send out (export) energy to the utility power grid, or charge its energy storage devices, such as batteries, via a bidirectional AC/DC converter. On the other hand, if the loads on the microgrid exceed its internal generation, the microgrid can either take energy from the utility grid or from its own charged energy storage sources. This is the grid-connected (normal) mode of operation. However, when a fault occurs on the utility grid and the load demands are not met, the microgrid disconnects itself from the utility grid at the PCC and begins to function in islanded mode. The merits of AC microgrids include its adaptability that makes it easier to be integrated with the original AC power infrastructure, and the simplicity of its voltage transformation. Also, the AC microgrid equipment costs less compared to DC microgrids. AC microgrids are a feasible option for both cities and rural areas. If disturbances or faults occur, reliable power can be generated in isolated mode. Consequently, as of today, the number of AC microgrids far exceeds that of DC microgrids.

Figure 25: Schematic of an Alternating Current Microgrid Bus with Solar and Wind Generation

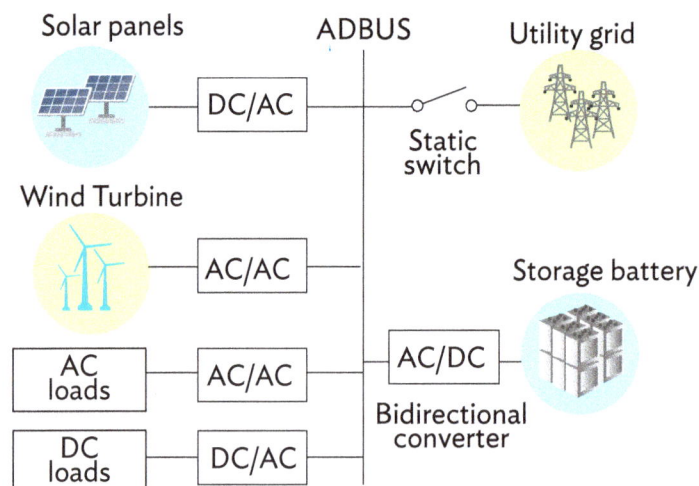

AC = alternating current, DC = direct current.
Source: Anam, F., A. A. Sahito, and A. Shah. 2018. *Comparison of AC and DC Microgrid Considering Solar-Wind Hybrid Renewable Energy System. Engineering Science and Technology International Research Journal.* 2(1). pp. 33–38. http://www.estirj.com/Volume.1/6Faiza21.pdf.

DC microgrid. The operating principle of a DC microgrid is similar to an AC microgrid, but it is connected to a DC bus. Similar to AC microgrids, DC microgrids can also be operated in grid-connected or isolated modes. Although it typically has a higher capital cost, the operating costs and system losses are usually lower due to direct connection to DC loads via single stage power conversion. DC microgrids are likely to see increased popularity in the coming years as it gives several operational advantages over AC microgrids. In DC microgrids, the generation and distribution system comprises mostly PV units, wind turbines, fuel cells, and other renewable energy sources used to meet energy demands. From its storage devices, it utilizes the DC output voltage, and voltage regulation is better. As there is no need for frequency control, additional system synchronization is not required.

Figure 26: Schematic Diagram of a Direct Current Microgrid using Solar, Wind, and Microgas Turbines

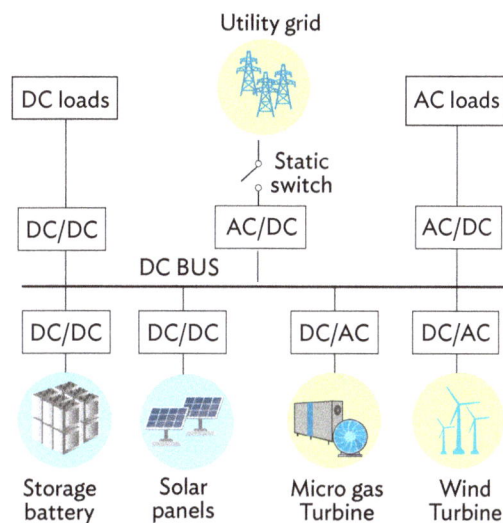

AC = alternating current, DC = direct current.

Note: **A hybrid AC/DC**. Hybrid microgrid is a combination of both AC and DC microgrid, bidirectional converters, and control equipment. Hybrid AC/DC microgrids offer the best solution for grid integration of different DER. A hybrid AC/DC microgrid has minimal conversion losses.

Source: Anam, F., A. A. Sahito, and A. Shah. 2018. *Comparison of AC and DC Microgrid Considering Solar-Wind Hybrid Renewable Energy System. Engineering Science and Technology International Research Journal.* 2(1). pp. 33–38. http://www.estirj.com/Volume.1/6Faiza21.pdf.

Figure 27: Typical Block Diagram of a Hybrid Alternating Current/Direct Current Microgrid

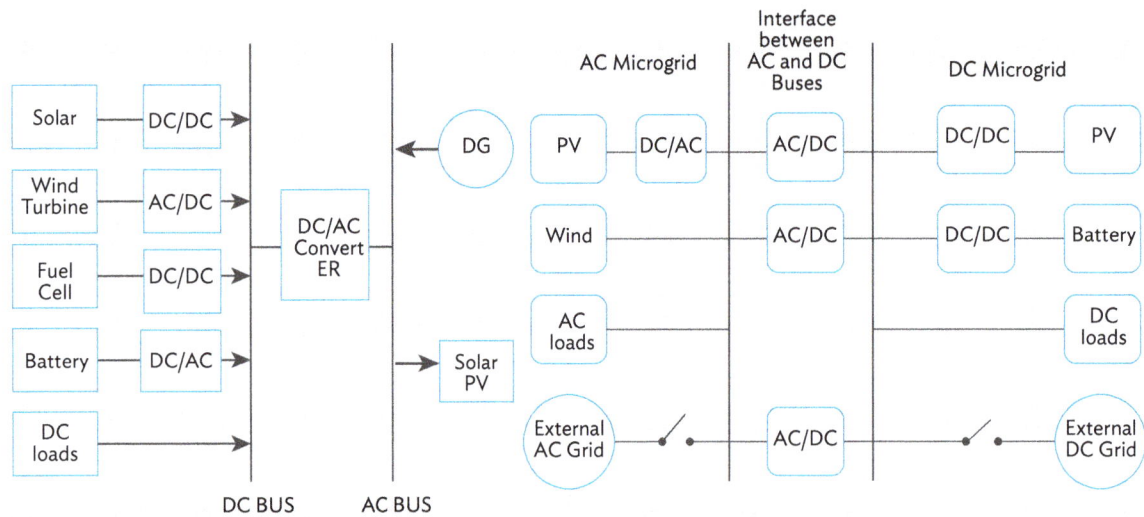

AC = alternating current, DC = direct current, PV = photovoltaic.

Notes:

1. Both the above schematics depict solar, wind, fuel cell as a source of energy and battery for power storage. The left diagram shows a hybrid single bus system with only DC loads; on the right side diagram is a hybrid two bus power supply system with AC and DC loads.

2. AC, DC, and hybrid microgrids each have distinct features, merits, and demerits (Table 5).

Source: Figures taken from Anam, F., A. A. Sahito, and A. Shah. 2018. Comparison of AC and DC Microgrid Considering Solar-Wind Hybrid Renewable Energy System. *Engineering Science and Technology International Research Journal*. 2(1). pp. 33–38. http://www.estirj.com/Volume.1/6Faiza21.pdf.

Table 5: Features of Microgrid Types (Alternating Current, Direct Current, and Hybrid)

Features	Description
Maturity level: Advantage – AC	• AC microgrid technologies are more mature than DC microgrid technologies and have existed for many years in some applications. However, with a growing market and evolving application landscape, areas for improvement continue to emerge in aspects such as new products, reduced cost, simplicity, and improved resilience. • AC-linked distributed energy systems completely dominate some segments as they are the only ones commercially available. Currently, DC-linked architectures are commercially available mainly in specific market segments such as remote area minigrids for small residential applications, such as those in India.
Efficiency: Advantage – DC	• With solar PV generation and energy storage growing rapidly in the microgrid mix, along with the ongoing shift toward DC loads such as energy-efficient LED lighting, there will be a strong case for interconnecting all these via DC power networks. In such case, DC microgrid architectures, on a building level at least, can reduce capital costs, and increase energy efficiency, reliability, and resilience.
Design simplicity: Advantage – DC	• DC microgrids typically involve less customization and are simpler to design (although capital cost may be higher, particularly in brownfield installations, owing to lesser reuse of existing, typically AC, equipment).

continued on next page

Table 5 *continued*

Features	Description
Simplicity of operation: Advantage – Hybrid	• DC microgrids provide numerous advantages over AC microgrids, such as removing the need for synchronization and frequency adjustment as well as appropriateness in supporting DC loads and distributed energy resources (DERs). As such, the most complicated of microgrid processes is decoupling (islanding) and reconnection to the main grid. DC microgrids can relatively simplify this islanding and reconnection process due to their separation from the main utility grid via DC–AC inverters. This results in better power quality on the microgrid. • However, this is an area for synergistic integration of AC and DC microgrids into hybrid microgrids with DC microgrid on sub-microgrid level, and AC microgrid on the main microgrid level. By decoupling loads on the DC side via DC–AC inverters, the main microgrid reduces the corresponding issues related to voltage, frequency and nonlinear loads, which are now "filtered" by the DC–AC inverters.

Other considerations for DC	• Merits
	  ° Plug-in approach for all DER
	  ° Well-developed interconnection, product standards, and codes
	  ° More end-use products are designed for use with AC low voltage electrical systems
	• Demerits
	  ° Increased conversion requirements from DC to AC and back to DC
	  ° Energy losses in the conversion
	  ° More equipment and devices required

Other considerations for DC	• Merits
	  ° DC produced and stored by PV systems, fuel cells, and batteries
	  ° DC used by increasing number of electrical devices
	  ° Lower conversion requirements
	  ° AC to DC conversion is easier and cheaper than DC to AC
	  ° Reduction in number of devices required (e.g., batteries chargers)
	  ° Energy savings around 5%–15%
	  ° Improvement in reliability as there are fewer points of failure
	  ° Suitable for zero-net energy buildings
	  ° Suitable for data centers
	• Demerits
	  ° Lack of existing applications for DC LV distribution systems
	  ° Current lack of approved standards and codes for DC LV equipment, distribution systems, and microgrids
	  ° Lack of familiarity with design of DC LV distribution systems
	  ° Lack of approved and recognized DC LV system architecture (e.g., common bus collecting and distributing power)
	  ° Different safety and protection practices compared with AC LV distribution systems
	  ° Infrastructure upgrade required from AC to DC

Other considerations for hybrid	• Merits
	  ° Suitable for applications where AC and DC power is produced and consumed
	  ° Similar operational benefits to DC microgrids
	• Demerits
	  ° Control of the system is more complicated than AC or DC

AC = alternating current, DC = direct current, DC LV = direct current low voltage, LED = light-emitting diode.

Note: Additional details are covered in Sections 1.7 (Operation) and 1.8 (Maintenance).

Source: Anam, F., A. A. Sahito, and A. Shah. 2018. *Comparison of AC and DC Microgrid Considering Solar-Wind Hybrid Renewable Energy System. Engineering Science and Technology International Research Journal.* 2(1). pp. 33–38. http://www.estirj.com/Volume.1/6Faiza21.pdf.

1.6 Design of a Microgrid

1.6.1 Phases in the Implementation of Microgrid Projects

From a project management perspective, the conceptualization, evaluation, design, construction, and commissioning of a microgrid follows the same broad stages as other infrastructure projects with similar stakeholders.

Figure 28: Lifecycle of a Microgrid Project Implementation

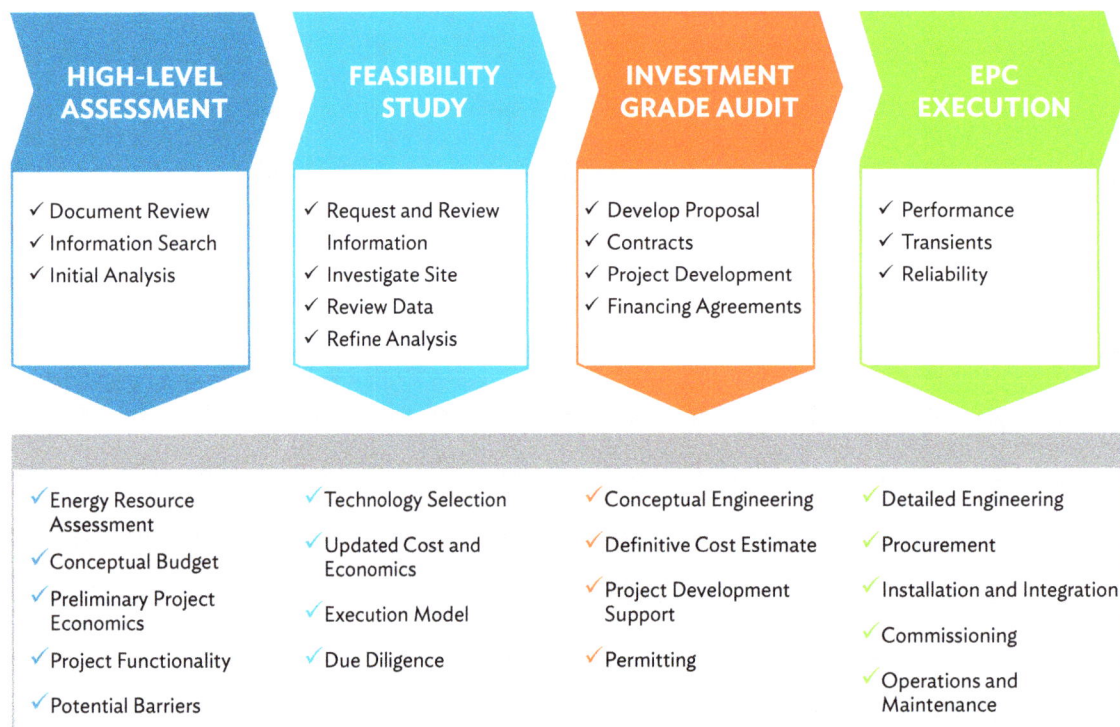

HIGH-LEVEL ASSESSMENT	FEASIBILITY STUDY	INVESTMENT GRADE AUDIT	EPC EXECUTION
✓ Document Review ✓ Information Search ✓ Initial Analysis	✓ Request and Review Information ✓ Investigate Site ✓ Review Data ✓ Refine Analysis	✓ Develop Proposal ✓ Contracts ✓ Project Development ✓ Financing Agreements	✓ Performance ✓ Transients ✓ Reliability
✓ Energy Resource Assessment ✓ Conceptual Budget ✓ Preliminary Project Economics ✓ Project Functionality ✓ Potential Barriers	✓ Technology Selection ✓ Updated Cost and Economics ✓ Execution Model ✓ Due Diligence	✓ Conceptual Engineering ✓ Definitive Cost Estimate ✓ Project Development Support ✓ Permitting	✓ Detailed Engineering ✓ Procurement ✓ Installation and Integration ✓ Commissioning ✓ Operations and Maintenance

EPC = engineering, procurement, and construction.
Source: Black and Veatch. 2016. *Microgrid Design & Execution Handbook: A consistent project approach for reliable results.* Black and Veatch. Kansas, USA.

In the case of an existing facility or brownfield microgrid, the pre-project evaluations begin with an assessment of the current situation. Both brownfield and greenfield projects would then undertake a high-level assessment (Figure 28) that includes:

(i)   Technical setup: current and historic levels of power supply reliability, current power generation mix, type of distribution grid, typical load profile, identification of critical loads versus controllable loads, heat and chill loads (if any), available space for a microgrid;

(ii)   Environmental considerations: emission rates, emission targets;

(iii)   Financial considerations: operating costs, fuel costs, electricity prices, fuel price volatility, proportion of electricity costs as a share of total cost of sold goods, opportunity costs of outages caused by historic levels of reliability; and

(iv)   Project objectives: minimize energy bills, reduce outages, reduce emissions, provide spinning reserve, peak demand reduction, etc.

The subsequent project feasibility study includes the following key considerations:

(i)   Applicable policies: planning and permitting regulations, power tariff structure, grid connection charges, grid use of system charges;

(ii)   Renewable resource: wind speeds, solar irradiation, shadow effects;

(iii)   Site information: land availability, thresholds that trigger planning permission, environmental impact assessment, visual impact assessment, timescales for development, supply chain lead times; commercial structures: self-ownership, infrastructure fund, independent power producer (IPP), power purchase agreement (PPA), returns to owners;

(iv)   Financing structure: balance sheet, debt/equity, PPP, etc.; and

(v)   Technical viability: grid integration principles, technology choices and optimum size, site layout, ability to feed power back to grid.

A summary of the social, economic, technical, and legal and regulatory criteria that need to be addressed as part of a microgrid's investment grade project evaluation is in Table 6.

Table 6: Social, Economic, Technical, and Legal and Regulatory Evaluation Criteria for Microgrids

	Criteria	Description
Social	Management	Ease of managing the electrfication system inside the families among them.
	Equity	Equality in the amount of electricity supplied to each family.
	Household benefits	Improvements in the quality of life of the families and their incomes.
	Community services	Electrification of the community services (school, health center, church).
	Productive activities	Generation of local jobs thanks to the development of productive activities.
	Impact on local resources	Land covered by the installed equipment.
	Clean energy	Renewables with the variable generation or hybrid.
Economic	Investment	The initial investment, operation, and maintenance costs.
	Tariff	The effort of consumers to pay the tariff for the electricity.
	Subsidies	Financial aid or support granted by the state or public or private authorities.
	Fuel Savings	Reduced losses, combined heat, cooling, and power, etc.
	Ancillary services	Congestion relief, frequency regulation, reactive power, and voltage control, etc.
Technical	Application	Campus, institutional, military, residential, remote, and/or rural areas.
	Supplied energy	Amount of energy and power supplied to each family.
	Continuity of the resources	Reliability of the used energy resources and autonomy of the batteries.
	Flexibility	Expandability of users and increase in consumption.
	Local replacement	Assiatance to repair equipment failure.
	Local manufacturing	The proximity to the places where the equipment is manufactured.
	Energy security	System reliabiity in the event of failures: equipment, service weather, cascading outages, cyber and physical attacks.
Legal and Regulatory	Regulatory issues	State or private regulation.
	Interconnection	Deregulation of small power producers, load aggregator.
	Utility regulation	Regulation by public or private authorities.

Source: Santos, A. Q. et al. 2018. Framework for Microgrid Design Using Social, Economic, and Technical Analysis. *Energies*. 11: 2832. doi:10.3390/en11102832. https://www.mdpi.com/1996-1073/11/10/2832.

1.6.2 Design Parameters

Once the feasibility study is completed and the project receives a green signal, the aspects to consider in the microgrid system design during subsequent conceptual and detailed engineering stages are listed below and pictured in the flowchart on Figure 29:

1. Demand forecasting

    (i)   Number of customers
    (ii)   Length of circuits
    (iii) Load analysis (e.g., critical, controllable, high efficiency, etc.)
           – Somewhat challenging in the case of low-income customers with limited technical and financial resources, hence, estimates and extrapolations may need to be used.

2. Generation capacity sizing

    (i)   Generation mix
    (ii)   DER sizing and design
           – Optimal sizing of PV and wind
    (iii) Nonrenewable generation sizing

3. Energy storage devices selection, combination, and sizing

    (i)   Standby power loss
           – Storage is primarily needed when the microgrid is islanded
           – Standby power loss will reduce the efficiency of the microgrid
    (ii)   Response time
           – For seamless transition, response time must be very fast
           – This is more than just battery response time –communications latency and control functions also play a role

4. Technical design

    (i)   Microgrid controller architecture and design
           – Centralized versus decentralized
    (ii)   Power technology
           – AC versus DC versus hybrid microgrids
    (iii) Voltage levels
    (iv)   Feeder configuration
    (v)   Desired power quality and reliability levels
    (vi)   Protection methods – Several protection schemes have been developed for AC microgrids, both centralized and decentralized. For DC microgrids, this area is less developed because of the lack of standards and guidelines, along with limited practical experience
    (vii) Communications technology
    (viii) Distribution system modeling, simulation, and design
           – Scenarios
           – Model validation
           – Grid impact
    (ix)   Impact studies
           – Steady state
           – Fault analysis
           – Protection
           – Stability studies

One critical consideration is building systems that can grow with the customers' increased socioeconomic improvement. It is important to select vendors with plug-and-play, modular designs that can be expanded, and are interoperable, backward compatible and forward integrable, as well as with open standards to the extent possible.

Figure 29: Microgrid Design Steps Flowchart

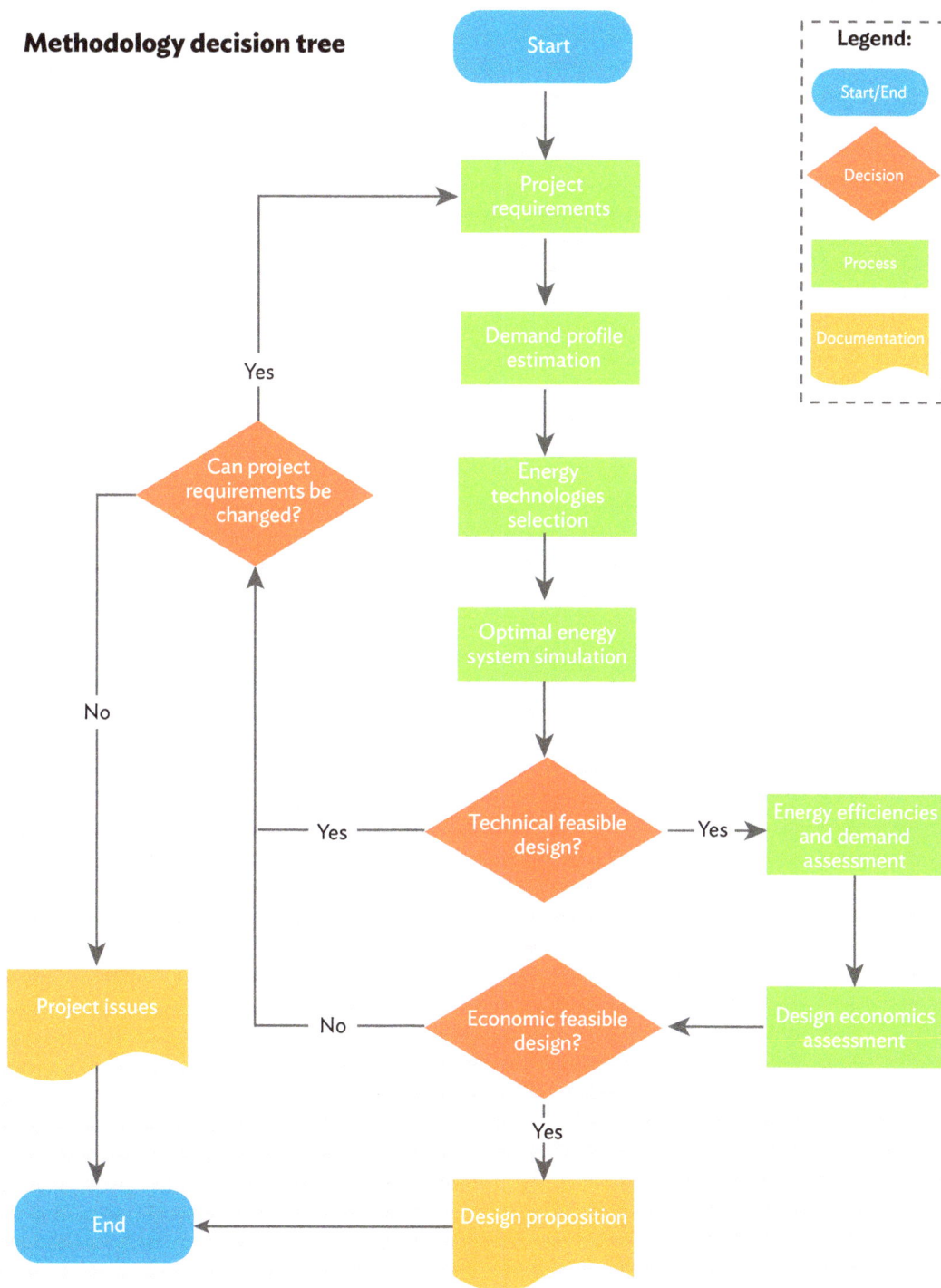

Source Santos, A. Q. et al. 2018. Framework for Microgrid Design Using Social, Economic, and Technical Analysis. *Energies.* 11: 2832. doi:10.3390/en11102832. https://www.mdpi. com/1996-1073/11/10/2832.

1.6.3 Design Software

Technical design of microgrids is a complex process taking into account multiple parameters listed in Section 1.6.2. Consequently, various models are required to understand a variety of microgrid operational, control, and integration aspects such as performance, grid interaction, and protection impact in a range of scenarios. Several software are available for this including those listed Appendixes 7 and 8.

1.6.4 Product Selection

Most of the components used in microgrids are commercially available today from several large vendors as well as several niche players. As volumes increase, price declines are likely, and continued improvements in performance and functionality can be expected. Several companies are also involved in the integration space (including the product suppliers themselves as well as engineering companies). Hence, once a microgrid is conceptualized and evaluated, its design, product, and integration services can follow standard procurement processes.

1.6.5 Capital Costs

A microgrid's total capital costs include those arising from its early stage development; feasibility studies; permitting, design; land acquisition; equipment purchase; engineering, procurement, and construction (EPC); and commissioning. These costs are likely to vary widely by application, the level reliability and, in turn, sophistication of the microgrid, and whether it is a greenfield site with no existing equipment or brownfield site with existing assets, as well as, to an extent, by geography. However, by far the largest component appears to be cost of the distributed generation equipment, followed by the microgrid control system. Figure 30 shows the average per-MW installed capital cost of microgrids in the United States based on a 2016 study (Giraldez et al. 2018).

Figure 30: United States Microgrid Costs, by Segment

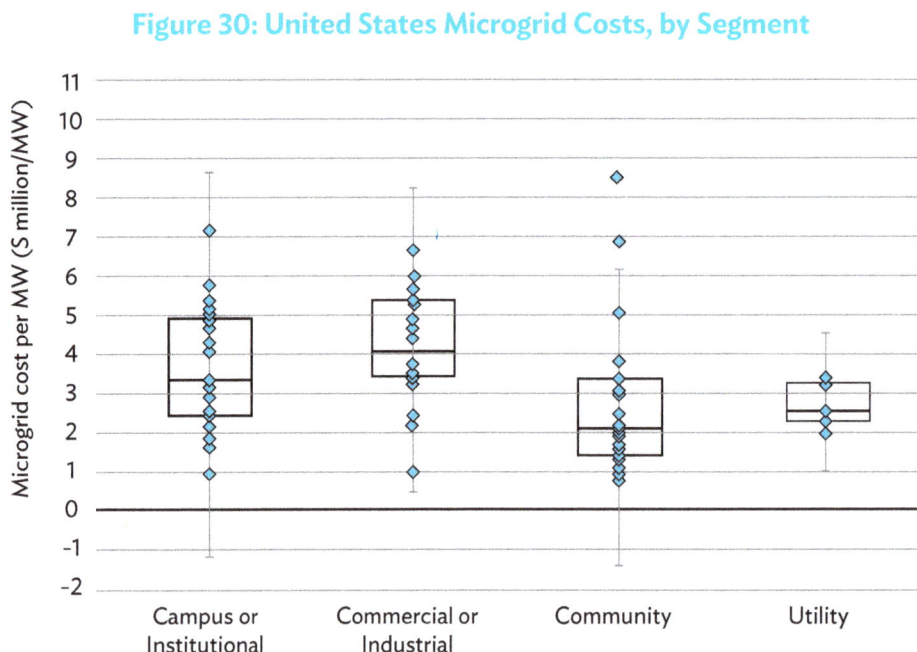

MW = megawatt.

Note: The box chart shows the interquartile range (IQR) and mean of 80 analyzed US microgrid sites in US dollars as of 2016.

Source: Giraldez, J., et al. 2018. *Phase I Microgrid Cost Study: Data Collection and Analysis of Microgrid Costs in the United States.* National Renewable Energy Laboratory (NREL), Juwi Americas, and Navigant Consulting. www.nrel.gov/publications.

1.7   Microgrid Operations and Maintenance

There are two operating modes for a grid-connected microgrid. The normal operating mode is the grid-connected mode. In this operating mode all the feeders are supplied by the utility or main grid, and the microgrid typically operates this way as long as there is no power quality disturbance on main grid. However, when there is a fault of other power disturbance on the main grid, the microgrid will be disconnected from it (in a planned or unplanned manner). This is referred to as "islanded" or "isolated" mode of operation. Such transitions, along with maintaining of system stability and fault detection are three critical areas for proper microgrid operation.

1.7.1   Transition Between Grid-Connected and Islanded Modes

The ability to transfer between grid-connected and islanded modes without any interruptions to the customers is an important function. If certain load and distribution system conditions are foreseen that need to be managed in advance, such seamless transfers can ideally be initiated by the microgrid operator. If a storm warning has been issued, the microgrid operator may decide to the transfer the microgrid from grid-connected to islanded mode operation by simply by initiating the sequence via their control system. Once the storm has passed, the microgrid can resume grid-connected operation by seamlessly synchronizing back into the distribution system. In the case of unscheduled events such as distribution system faults however, there might be brief interruptions in supply to the microgrid's loads depending on the protection system type and setup. In the reverse operation, while reconnecting, the microgrid needs certain information from the grid for synchronization, particularly voltage and frequency setpoints. With the right controls, synchronization can be achieved relatively quickly, typically in a few seconds, thus making islanding (at least in the case of planned transitions) and reconnection operations seamless, and thereby eliminating the brief outages that might otherwise affect critical end-user loads.

1.7.2   Maintaining Microgrid System Stability and Synchronous Operation

The main power grid dictates the overall system dynamics while in grid-connected mode, due to the much smaller size of microgrids. Thus, the stability analysis of a microgrid in grid-connected mode is similar to that of the larger power grid to which it is connected. Conversely, in an islanded microgrid operation, the system dynamics are represented by the DGs, the fluctuating output of which, coupled with varying load, may pose challenges to the successful operation of the microgrid. Three levels of supervisory control are typically employed for the reliable operation of a microgrid in grid-connected mode—the distribution level, microgrid level, and local level. The market operator and distribution network operator (DNO) are involved at distribution level. MCC handles microgrid level control, and the unit level control is done by local controllers (Faisal and Islam 2017). At the distribution level, signals are dispatched by DNO and market operator. MCC handles communications between DNO and local controller to integrate the microgrid with the main grid. Microgrid supervisory control can be decentralized or centralized as described in an earlier section of this handbook. Appendix 5 lists a comparison between AC and DC microgrid control strategies.

When a microgrid is operating in grid-connected mode, the utility provides a convenient, reliable reference for voltage and frequency to maintain microgrid synchronous operation—i.e., the utility is the isochronous[12] generator reference and all DG and storage resources operate in droop[13] mode. However, when it is islanded from the grid, it needs to rely on its own internal assets to provide this reference to independently support power quality and accommodate any changes to system voltage levels. Currently, many islanded microgrids employ

---

[12]   Isochronous control mode means that the frequency (and voltage) of the electricity generated is held constant, and there is zero generator droop.

[13]   Droop control mode is a strategy commonly applied to generators for voltage and frequency control to allow parallel generator operation for load sharing.

thermal or NG generators that operate as synchronous machines to provide that isochronous reference, as well as supply reactive power and dynamically regulate system voltages, while other generators, PV invertors, and sometimes, battery invertors operate in droop mode. However, an additional challenge exists for islanded microgrids operating with a significant amount of renewable generation. Such systems are typically completely inverter-based and lack any spinning generators. Therefore, they must rely on an intelligent inverter coupled with battery storage, which will operate in voltage and frequency control mode to provide its own reference points, as well as in conjunction with other devices like static compensators (STATCOM) to supply fast-acting continuous voltage regulation. Managing this process is one of the core control functionalities of a fully renewable microgrid (ABB 2016).

1.7.3   Faults

An electric fault in lay terms is an abnormal current on the grid, something that can result from a variety of reasons including short circuits. Traditional utility grid methods of fault detection do not apply to microgrids due to the bi-directionality of power flow, the need to distinguish between gird-connected and islanded operation modes, and that converters interfacing the DERs provide limited fault current compared to some of the equipment and machinery that might be on the microgrid. Fault detection and design of protection systems are extremely critical areas for microgrids, and currently, there is no standard one-size-fits-all solution. The design-and-process is typically customized to the individual microgrid with several methods or combinations used including differential protection, communications systems, and advanced signal processing algorithms.

1.7.4   Operational Costs

Operational costs in a microgrid can vary widely, but typically have fixed and variable components. Considering strictly operational costs, i.e., excluding maintenance costs, the fixed costs usually accrue mainly from staff salaries, and general and administrative expenses; and the variable costs from energy generation—the latter being essentially the total cost of electricity supplied by the microgrid to its end users. The effective total cost of energy in the microgrid is, therefore, the cost of generation by each source in the microgrid (based on LCOE of the constituent generating DERs), plus the energy purchased from the utility, minus any payment received from the utility for exported electricity and grid services provided to it (by the control of dispatchable generation sources and DSM of controllable flexible loads). This implies that the microgrid's operational costs greatly depend on optimal design of the microgrid's generation mix, and leveraging the economic dispatch of each of these functions during operation.

1.7.5   Maintenance

As in the case of any other product or system or infrastructure, regular maintenance and upkeep is essential to ensure reliable performance over the effective service life of a microgrid. Fixed costs (e.g., maintenance staff salaries) and variable costs (e.g., direct variable costs that include replacement component costs, and indirect variable costs that include substitute backup generation during maintenance shutdown periods) will be incurred for this. The maintenance strategy and procedures of a microgrid are typically carried out by O&M personnel, based on established protocols and intervals such as periodic general maintenance, scheduled preventive maintenance, and data analytics-based predictive maintenance. Given that there are several different microgrid applications, with varying service requirements and grid connectivity scenarios, there is no one-size-fits-all prescription, and the maintenance costs need to be compared to the cost of failure disruption, potential for risk reduction, and reliability enhancement, to yield a quantified financial metric, such as percentage or absolute risk reduction per dollar or expense and/or investment.

The maintenance activities and costs in a microgrid are essentially those of its individual components such as renewable or nonrenewable distributed generation sources, batteries, microgrid control system, sensors, communication networks, distribution system, protection equipment, transformers, and electrical components. For instance, the maintenance procedures for solar PV systems are available in detail from relevant sources, with its annual maintenance cost usually being about 2% of its capital cost.

Like most in operational plants, O&M activities could be do-it-yourself, or entrusted to an O&M contractor, or handled by the integrator who built the plant—each has its pros and cons (Figure 31). This aspect often comes up at the financing stage as part of due diligence on the overall capabilities and credibility of the microgrid developer and operator.

Figure 31: Operation and Maintenance Contractor Options

DO-IT-YOURSELF	O&M CONTRACTOR	YOUR INTEGRATOR
You manage the day-to-day operations and fix problems if they arise.	Some companies specialize in monitoring systems.	The people who engineered and built your microgrid will also run it.
PROS: Often less expensive, and you're onsite if something were to go wrong **CONS:** Complexity usually requires training and staff dedicated to the microgrid	**PROS:** Cost-competitive and frees up your time **CONS:** Still a learning curve for a third party to understand your particular microgrid, or their sense of urgency may not be the same as yours	**PROS:** They built your microgrid, so they know it best, and their trained staff will be quickest to resolve any issues **CONS:** There's only one option—the people who built your system
QUESTIONS TO CONSIDER:	**QUESTIONS TO CONSIDER:**	**QUESTIONS TO CONSIDER:**
• How do I need to train my staff—both when the project comes online and then continually to carry over knowledge during staff turnover? • Do I need more staff to dedicate to monitoring the microgrid?	• Are you prepared to on-board a third party and explain how your microgrid is setup? • Are you sure contractors are knowledgeable in microgrid complexity, or will this system be too difficult for them?	• Who do you want on the other end of the line when you need help? • Did your EPC scope involve post-installation operations and maintenance?

EPC = engineering, procurement, and construction; O&M = operation and maintenance.

Source: S&C Electric. 2018. *The Long- and Short-Term Care of Your Microgrid.* https://www.sandc.com/globalassets/ sac-electric/ documents/sharepoint/documents---all-documents/educational-material-180-4506. pdf?dt=637212583873651116.

Box 1: Demonstration and Deployment Case 1

Case Study: Weymouth Water Treatment Plant in La Verne, California, United States

Location	La Verne, California
Country	United States
Year of Commissioning	2015
Asset Owner	The Metropolitan Water District of Southern California
Water Treatment Capacity	520 million gallons (1.97 billion liters) per day
Renewable Energy Technology	Solar PV
Renewable Energy Installation Size	3 MW
Business Model	Up-front Capital Investment by Consumer
Grid Connection	Grid-connected
Average Electricity Consumption	~14.4 million kWh per annum
Total Electricity Generated by the Solar Plant per Annum	6.5 million kWh per annum (45% of the water treatment plant's overall electricity consumption)
Tracking System	Total of 539 sun-tracking stations, each supporting a string of 20 315-watt panels. The tracking systems will produce 25% more power than fixed panels.
Capital Expenditure of 3 MW Solar PV System	$10.5 million
Business Model	Up-front Capital Investment by Consumer
Total Electricity Generated per Annum	~6.5 million kWh per annum
Estimated Cost Savings per Annum	~ $1 million
Simple Payback Period	~10 Years

kWH = kilowatt-hour, MW = megawatt, PV = photovoltaic.

Project Sponsor

California has been a leader among US states in adopting and supporting renewable energy and energy efficiency practices. One such adoption has been demonstrated by Southern California's Metropolitan Water District (MWD). The MWD of Southern California is a public institution established in 1928 to provide reliable water supply to the population (~18 million currently) living within a 5,200 square mile service area within six counties. One of the metropolitan's largest treatment plants is the F. E. Weymouth Water Treatment Plant (Weymouth), a 520 million-gallon-per-day (mgd) facility located in the City of La Verne. Weymouth plant consumed over 10 million kWh of electricity in 2013, and this demand for energy at the plant had increased by over 30% to about 14.4 million kWh by 2016.

Key Considerations

(i)   **Protection against fluctuations in retail electricity markets.** The fossil fuels-based retail electricity market is becoming more volatile due to competition for global natural resources available and increased regulations on carbon emissions.

(ii) **Climate change concerns.** The electricity procured from retail grid utilities in the region is generated from a combination of fossil fuels and hydropower. As climate change increasingly challenges water reliability, the MWD wanted the greater part of its energy consumption to come from the clean energy solutions.

(iii) **Prior experience with renewables.** The project sponsor had prior experience of successfully building and operating renewable energy assets for water treatment. The project owner has already in execution two renewable energy assets—a 1 MW solar plant at its Robert A. Skinner Water Treatment Plant in Southwest Riverside County and a 10.5 MW facility at Diamond Valley Lake Visitor Center in Hemet.

continued on next page

Box 1 *continued*

Project Description

The 3 MW Weymouth Solar Power installation generates 6.5 million kWh of clean electricity annually. This is consumed onsite and supplies nearly 45% of electricity required to treat water at the site. As a result, consumption of electricity from the grid utility, Southern California Edison, has been reduced significantly at Weymouth, saving energy costs, and reducing greenhouse gas emissions associated with the treatment of water at Weymouth. The solar plant has reduced an estimated $1 million in annual energy costs of the water treatment plant.

The 3 MW solar power generation facility is ground-mounted and includes a single-axis tracking system that allows the installed panels to track the sun's path from east to west on daily basis. Approximately 15 acres of land space is used by the installation.

Business Model and Commercial Details

The 3 MW solar PV installation was built by the project owner on up-front capital investment model—i.e., the project sponsor invested its own capital resources. The energy generated by the solar installation is used to offset the energy consumption from the grid. The project sponsor will generate return on the capital invested through cost savings realized by replacing expensive electricity purchased on the retail market with captive clean energy generation.

In addition to achieving long-term cost savings, the microgrid installation is estimated to reduce 1,900+ tons of carbon dioxide emissions every year.

Sources: Metropolitan Water District of Southern California (MWDH), US. n.d. *Solar Power: Metropolitan's Investment in Renewable Energy*. http://www.mwdh2o.com/PDF_NewsRoom/solar_7%2025%20final.pdf.; and Scauzillo, S. 2016. Metropolitan Water District: Saving Money Lost during Drought by Investing in Solar. San Gabriel Valley Tribune. 10 August 2016. Updated: 30 August 2017. https://www.sgvtribune. com/2016/08/10/metropolitan-water-district-saving-money-lost-during-drought-by-investing-in-solar/.

Box 2: Demonstration and Deployment Case 2

Case Study: 750 kW ABB Microgrid Longmeadow Park in Johannesburg, South Africa

Location	Longmeadow, Johannesburg
Country	South Africa
Year of Commissioning	2016
Asset Owner	ABB is the owner, project developer, and end user
Microgrid Technology	• Microgrid Plus Control System • Solar PV (1 x 750 kWp) • PowerStore Battery (1 MW/380 kWh) • Diesel (2 x 600 kW) • Remote Monitoring
Renewable Energy Installation Capacity	750 kW
Business Model	Up-front Capital Investment by Consumer
Grid Connection	Grid-connected
Project Benefits	• Cut annual diesel fuel consumption by 27% • Cut annual diesel generator use by 76% • Cut energy costs by $150,000 per year or 33%, to $460,000 • Reduce overall carbon emissions by an estimated 1,000 tons per year.
Capital Expenditure of Microgrid	~$1.22 million
Installation Model	Up-front Capital Investment by Consumer
Estimated Cost Savings per Annum	~$150,000
Simple Payback Period	~8 years

kW = kilowatt, MW = megawatt.

Box 2 *continued*

Project Background

In the Sub-Saharan Africa region, South Africa is the highest consumer of electricity. Within South Africa, 41% of the demand comes from private sector companies. However, the supply of electricity often falls short of demand. As a result, government has introduced peak demand charges to disincentivize consumption of electricity during particular times of the day when utilities are not able to meet high power demand. Along with this, there are also frequent power cuts. Consequently, many companies have turned to diesel generators for reliable back-up power supply. This causes increased energy costs and reliance on polluting fossil fuels.

Key Considerations

(i)   Quality of electricity is a major challenge for a manufacturing setup. With its round-the-clock operational hours, there can major financial implications if there are power cuts or fluctuating power supply. An ABB facility in Longmeadow, Johannesburg faced one power cut every 3 days, ~10 a month.

(ii)   The electricity supplied from grid is generally coal powered in South Africa and diesel gensets are the primary mode of power backup. This has led to over reliance on fossil fuels for ABB, which had four gensets in place prior to the installation of Solar photovoltaic (PV)-based microgrid.

(iii)   Being a global leader in providing energy solutions, ABB was also motivated to showcase a PV-based microgrid solution for its facility in Johannesburg. Having installed about 40 microgrids globally, it was only prudent for them to find a cleaner solution for their own needs.

(iv)   PV microgrid with battery storage also comes with its cost savings benefits that ABB wanted to realize.

Project Description

ABB has a 96,000-square-meter facility in Johannesburg that houses both the company's national headquarters and a manufacturing facility, with around 1,000 employees. Its electrical loads add up to roughly 1,000 kW, which are connected via a medium voltage grid connection to a local utility.

Four back-up diesel generators (two rated at 600 kilovolt-ampere [kVA] and two rated at 800 kVA) were being used since 2009 for power shortages and short-term voltage fluctuations. As a result of these two issues, its total energy cost in 2015 was $630,00 including utility charges and diesel fuel costs.

To overcome the challenge, ABB designed a microgrid solution that included a control system and 750 kWp rooftop solar PV system with the support of a 1 megavolt-ampere (MVA)/ 380 kWh PowerStore Battery based on lithium-ion (Li-ion) technology. The number of diesel gensets reduced to two 600 kVA diesel generators. This is grid-connected microgrid that can island and go off-grid as needed.

Business Model and Commercial Details

The primary financial driving factor for this ABB microgrid was cost savings. With this new microgrid, it was estimated that diesel consumption would be reduced by 27%, running time for generators would be reduced by 75%—from 433 hours to 106 hours. This effectively would lead to a reduction in energy costs from $610,000 to $460,000 per annum. That translates into a cost saving of ~25%.

In addition to achieving long-term cost savings, the microgrid installation is estimated to reduce 1,000+ tons of carbon dioxide emissions every year.

Source: ABB. 2017. *ABB Microgrids Case Study—Longmeadow*. South Africa. http://search.abb.com/library/Download.aspx?DocumentID=9AKK107045A3118&LanguageCode=en&DocumentPartId=LoRes&Action=Launch.

2 Business Models and Financial Analysis

2.1 Business Model for Grid-Connected Microgrids (Including Technology, Financing, Stakeholders)

Business models and financial and economic analyses are necessary to arrive at an appropriate investment and scale-up structure for grid-connected microgrids. The following business models are typically employed for microgrids to meet relevant pricing options and financing implications:

(i) customer-owned (up-front capital investment)
(ii) renewable energy service company (RESCO)-owned
(iii) utility-owned
(iv) cooperative-owned
(v) community-owned
(vi) pay-as-you-go (PayGo – typically rural remote minigrids)
(vii) remote (non-grid connected)

Key considerations for business model evaluation and selection are:

(i) availability of capable and experienced RESCOs locally and their interest in implementing clean energy microgrids in addition to their preferred business-implementation-investment model;
(ii) security of financial flows to the investor or financier;
(iii) cost and flexibility to end user and market demand and alignment;
(iv) LCOE;
(v) internal rate of return, net present value, and debt service coverage ratio of various business models;
(vi) international best practices and local affordability;
(vii) regulatory barriers and enablers such as requirements for a private entity to obtain electricity generation and distribution license from the government; and
(viii) stakeholder mapping to determine each of their roles and responsibilities.

Financial analysis will help

(i) determine if a financial investment in the renewable energy asset for a particular site is feasible,
(ii) determine the business model that provides the highest cost savings to the relevant stakeholder or investor (RESCO or an investor or consumers), and
(iii) demonstrate potential risks to future revenues or debt servicing and to quantify these risks through sensitivity analyses.

2.2 Business Model Evaluation and Selection

Choice of business model, through which the microgrid asset shall be built, operated, and maintained, is an important pre-development consideration irrespective of technology choice. Business model choices are typically between up-front capital investment model and the RESCO model. Within the RESCO model, variations exist, such as build-own-operate (BOO), build-own-operate-transfer (BOOT), lease-to-own, and PPA models. Among others, the two key considerations in the choice of business model are:

(i)   responsibility of making up-front capital expenditure investments for the microgrid asset, and

(ii)   responsibility of carrying out O&M throughout the useful life of the microgrid asset.

Table 7: Business Models for Microgrids

Business Models	Capital Expenditure Investment	Technology Risk	Asset Ownership	O&M Responsibility	Contracting Modalities Employed
Customer-owned (Up-front Capital Investment)	Borne by end energy consumer	Borne by end energy consumer	With end energy consumer	Borne by end energy consumer (but often outsourced to a third-party O&M contractor)	• EPC is performed by a third-party service provider (EPC contractor). The consumer generates financial benefits on its investment through cost savings
RESCO-owned	Borne by RESCO	Borne by RESCO	With RESCO; can be transferred to off taker depending upon the contract modality	Borne by RESCO	• Build-Own-Operate (BOO) • Build-Own-Operate-Transfer (BOOT) • Lease-to-own • Microgrid as a Service (MaaS) model • Power Purchase Agreement (PPA) model
Utility-owned	Borne by local utility	Borne by local utility	With the local utility	In-house or third-party service provider	• BOO • PPA
Cooperative-owned	Borne by local cooperative (often a cooperative of local electricity consumers – typically commercial and industrial consumers)	Borne by local cooperative or third-party developer	With local cooperative	Third-party service provider	• BOO • PPA • MaaS model

continued on next page

Table 7 *continued*

Business Models	Capital Expenditure Investment	Technology Risk	Asset Ownership	O&M Responsibility	Contracting Modalities Employed
Community-owned	Borne by local community (often deployed for a community of individual retail/residential consumers) or local utility	Borne by local community or local utility	With local community or local utility	Third-party service provider or local utility	• BOO • PPA • MaaS model
Pay-as-you-go (PayGo – typically rural remote minigrids)	Borne by investors	Borne by investors	With investors	Third-party service provider	• BOO • Lease-to-own • PPA
Remote (non-grid connected)	Borne by local community or local utility	Borne by local community or local utility	With local community or local utility	Third-party service provider or local utility	• Anchor-Business-Consumer model • BOO

EPC = engineering, procurement, and construction; O&M = operation and maintenance; RESCO = renewable energy service company.
Source: ADB.

A detailed description of all these models can be found in Appendix 10.

2.3 Financial Analysis

A financial and economic analysis of microgrids requires a study of their benefits and costs to the microgrid owner or operator and the utility or DNO (Figure 32).

Figure 32: Classification of the Costs Related to Microgrids

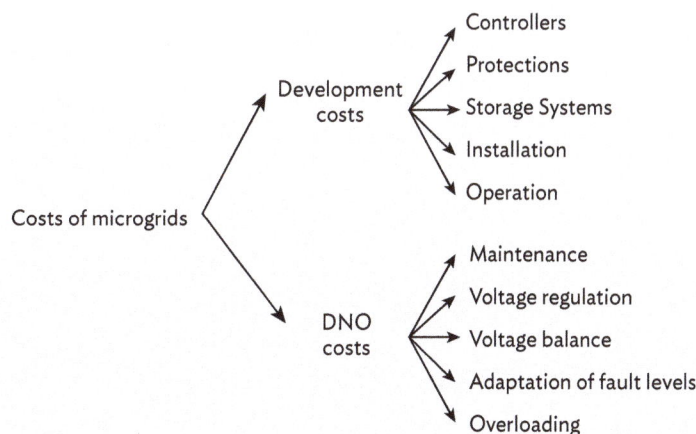

DNO = distribution network operator.
Source: Planas, E. et.al. 2015. *AC and DC Technology in Microgrids: A Review. Renewable and Sustainable Energy Reviews*. 43: pp. 726–749. https://doi.org/10.1016/j.rser.2014.11.067.

The key parameters for the financial analysis are listed below:

(i)   capital costs

(ii)   O&M costs

(iii)   LCOE

(iv)   revenue streams and qualitative analysis of benefits

(v)   financial and economic returns

(vi)   return on investment and payback period

(vii)   funding sources and structures

     (a)   monitoring of project outcomes

     (b)   tailored financial instruments

(viii) basic analysis methodology and examples of financial and economic analysis for each business model.

Revenue streams accruing from a microgrid are shown in Figure 33.

Figure 33: Components of Microgrid Value

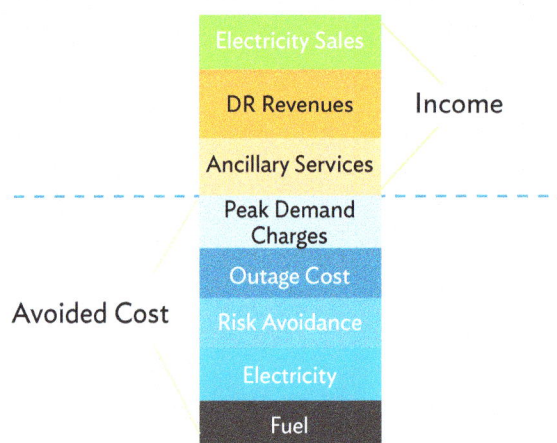

DR = demand-response.

Source: GTM Research. 2014. *North American Microgrids 2014: The Evolution of Localized Energy Optimization*. Boston, MA: GreenTech Media.

MICROGRID VALUE = AVOIDED COST + INCOME – CAPITAL COSTS – OPERATING COSTS

Microgrid value is typically shared among utilities, end users, third parties, or co-owners depending on the ownership and operating model. For instance,

(i)   In universities and public institutions, income streams arise from a large variety of loads that, if controlled, allow for DR and grid services. Avoided costs accrue from reduction in potential outage cost given the high reliability needs for research facilities and public safety facilities (such as airports and public transportation).

(ii)   Commercial and industrial units often do not create significant income streams, but the avoided costs accrue from a high demand charge reduction potential and reduction in potential outage cost (such as lost revenues and manufacturing delays).

Since all of the business models described in the previous section can be largely categorized either under up-front capital investment model or RESCO model, this financial analysis section focuses mainly on these two models. Both models will achieve cost savings (to varying degrees) to the consumer.

In the up-front capital investment model, the consumer makes the up-front investment, but all the electricity generated by the renewable energy asset is essentially free. Such a model involves

  (i)   one-time, large cash outflow – capital expenditure,
  (ii)   smaller but recurring cash outflows – O&M,
  (iii) larger but periodic cash outflows – equipment replacement cost, and
  (iv)   recurring cash inflows in the form of cost savings – total cost of electricity generated that the consumer would have otherwise paid to the grid electricity utility or for operating diesel generators in the absence of microgrid asset.

On the other hand, in the RESCO model, the consumer does not make any up-front investment, but will pay for use of electricity generated by the renewable energy asset as per the agreement with the RESCO. Such a model involves

  (i)   recurring cash outflows – price that the consumer will pay for electricity to the RESCO, as agreed in a PPA or lease or similar contract;
  (ii)   recurring cash inflows in the form of cost savings – discount in the price per kWh of electricity (if a PPA is signed) or general reduction in monthly electricity usage costs when compared to grid electricity or diesel generators (whichever is applicable as baseline).

Since cash outflows and inflows—both quantum and frequency of occurrence—significantly vary between the two models, the methodology used to conduct financial analysis also varies.

2.3.1 Financial Analysis Methodology for Up-Front Capital Investment Model and Renewable Energy Service Company

Table 8 presents the summary of the methodology for financial analysis for both up-front capital investment and RESCO models.

Table 8 : Summary of Financial Feasibility Methodology

Steps involved		Outputs
Collection of data		Capital costs, operating and maintenance costs, etc.
Selection of business model for the site		Up-front capital investment model of RESCO model (and selection of a variant such as build-own-operate or build-own-operate-transfer, in addition to contracting modality)
Financial analysis	**Up-front capital investment model**	Model inputs defined Net present value (NPV) Financial internal rate of return (FIRR) Benefits-to-cost ratio Payback period Sensitivity analysis
	RESCO model	Model inputs defined NPV Benefits-to-cost ratio Percentage of present value determined over period Sensitivity analysis
Finalizing the business model and presenting the results and/or benefits		NPV, benefits-to-cost ratio and other applicable metrics such as FIRR, payback period

RESCO = renewable energy service company.

Source: ADB.

Net Present Value Methodology

The NPV methodology is a useful financial tool to identify the feasibility of financial investments and to quantify the financial benefits to the investor. NPV is the difference between present value of cash inflows and present value of cash outflows over a period of time due to an investment. The formula is:

NPV = Present Value (Cash inflows) – Present Value (Cash outflows)

In short, the NPV methodology computes total gain or total loss that an investor stands to incur, in today's currency value, factoring in time value of money. If the NPV of an investment is positive, then the investment is considered to be value accretive, and hence, the proposed project investment can be approved. On the other hand, if NPV of an investment is negative, then the investment is considered to be value destructive and hence, the proposed project investment should be rejected, or other modalities such as capital subsidies need to be explored. If the NPV is 0, then the project investment is neither accretive nor destructive.

Financial Internal Rate of Return Methodology

Financial internal rate of return (FIRR) provides the rate at which a project generates financial return to its investors. Similar to the NPV methodology, the FIRR methodology also accounts for time value of money. But instead of presenting the output as a value in today's currency value, the FIRR methodology instead provides an easy to use percentage (%) based return calculation metric.

In general, if the FIRR is higher than the weighted average cost of capital of the project owner or investor, then the project is considered to be value accretive. On the other hand, if the FIRR is lower than the average cost of capital of the project owner, the project is considered to be value destructive.

Using Sensitivity Analysis

Although FIRR and NPV methodologies are widely used while taking project finance decisions around the world, sometimes the actual results may vary from estimations and projections. The variations are a result of the assumptions that are used to calculate NPV and FIRR values. When the assumptions made deviate from actuals, the resultant NPV and FIRR values also deviate.

Hence, it is prudent that a sensitivity analysis is carried out and that results of this sensitivity analysis are also a part of the decision-making process. A sensitivity analysis provides a narrow set of possibilities for NPV and FIRR, should the key inputs deviate from initial assumptions.

Process for Financial Analysis

Figure 34 depicts the process that will be followed in the financial feasibility analysis methodology for both up-front capital investment model and RESCO models.

Figure 34: Process Chart for Financial Analysis

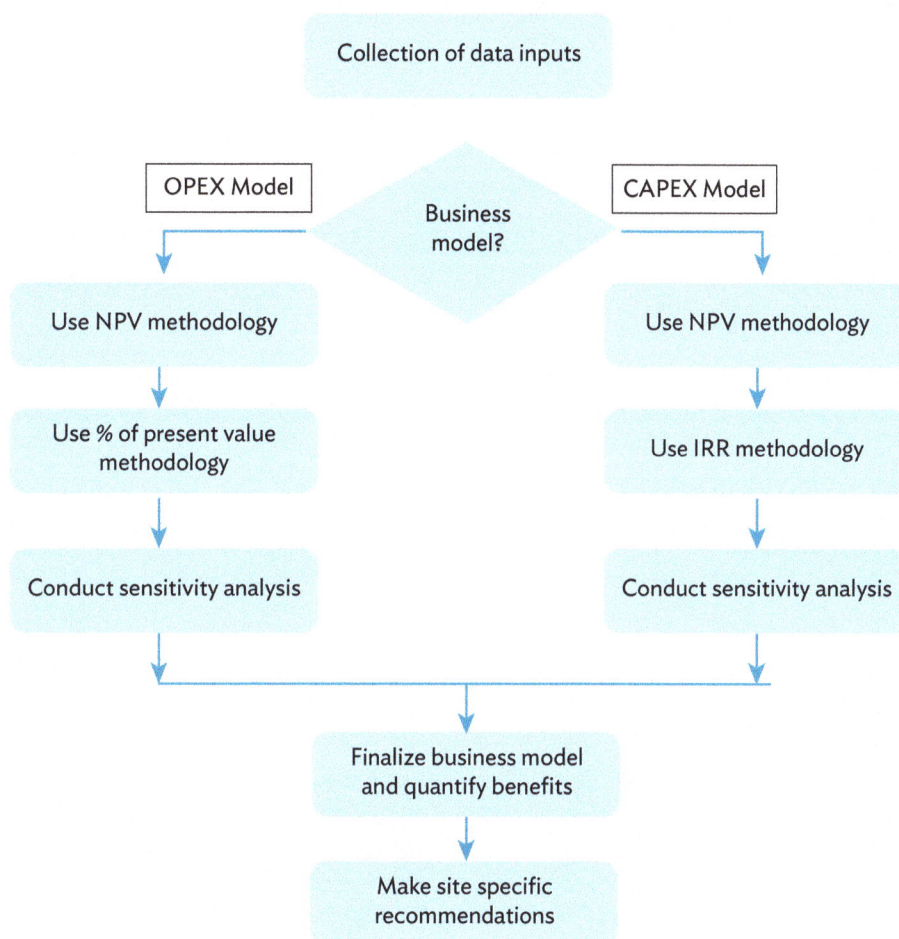

```
                    ┌─────────────────────┐
                    │ Collection of data inputs │
                    └─────────────────────┘

   ┌────────────┐         Business         ┌────────────┐
   │ OPEX Model │          model?          │ CAPEX Model │
   └────────────┘                          └────────────┘
         │                                        │
         ▼                                        ▼
  ┌──────────────────┐                   ┌──────────────────┐
  │ Use NPV methodology │                │ Use NPV methodology │
  └──────────────────┘                   └──────────────────┘
         │                                        │
         ▼                                        ▼
  ┌──────────────────┐                   ┌──────────────────┐
  │ Use % of present value │             │ Use IRR methodology │
  │ methodology        │                 └──────────────────┘
  └──────────────────┘                            │
         │                                        ▼
         ▼                                ┌──────────────────┐
  ┌──────────────────┐                    │ Conduct sensitivity analysis │
  │ Conduct sensitivity analysis │        └──────────────────┘
  └──────────────────┘
                        │
                        ▼
             ┌──────────────────────┐
             │ Finalize business model │
             │ and quantify benefits  │
             └──────────────────────┘
                        │
                        ▼
             ┌──────────────────────┐
             │ Make site specific    │
             │ recommendations       │
             └──────────────────────┘
```

CAPEX = capital expenditure, IRR = internal rate of return, NPV = net present value, OPEX = operating expense.
Source: ADB.

2.3.2 Inputs for Financial Analysis Model for Up-Front Capital Investment Model

In the up-front capital investment model, NPV and FIRR are the two parameters or metrics that are best suited to decide if the investment is financially beneficial to consumers, and quantify the financial savings that the consumer stands to generate by switching to renewable energy from their existing source of electricity (grid or diesel generators).

To conduct a financial feasibility analysis based on NPV and FIRR, the following operational and cash flow-specific inputs are required.

Operational Inputs

(i) number of units (kWh) of electricity generated per annum by the proposed renewable energy asset;
(ii) annual degradation factor (%) in output of proposed renewable energy asset;
(iii) cash outflows;
(iv) capital cost, either in total or in cost per Wp or kW of main electricity generating equipment (solar PV modules, etc.);
(v) balance of systems including inverters, batteries (if any), transformers (if any), T&D lines, charge controllers, as applicable;
(vi) cost of civil works, logistics, labor, etc. as applicable, apart from applicable taxes and duties;
(vii) annual O&M expense;
(viii) inflation-adjusted replacement cost of key components such as batteries and inverters as applicable;
(ix) inflation-adjusted cost of spares and repairs expected;
(x) insurance cost; and
(xi) dismantling cost of the system.

Cash Inflows (in case of existing power source = grid)

(i) current price per unit (kWh) of electricity consumed from the grid, including peak/off-peak consumption tariffs and average consumption in kWh at each of these tariff categories;
(ii) monthly/annual fixed charges based on connected load, if any;
(iii) grid usage and other charges, as applicable;
(iv) average expected increase in price per unit (kWh) of electricity, based on historical averages and market-based projections; and
(v) other charges, taxes and levies in connection to maintenance of the grid connection, if any.

2.3.3 Inputs for Financial Analysis Model for Renewable Energy Service Company Model

In the RESCO model, NPV methodology is best suited to decide if the investment is financially beneficial to the consumers as well as the RESCO and quantify the financial savings that consumers stand to generate by switching to renewable energy from baseline source of electricity (grid or diesel generators).

To conduct a financial feasibility analysis based on NPV methodology, the cash flow-specific inputs mentioned below are required.

Cash Outflows

(i) price per unit (kWh) of electricity as agreed in a PPA or lease payments agreed in a lease-to-own agreement;
(ii) escalation per annum (or any other period as agreed, in percent) in PPA unit price as part of the escalation clause in the PPA, if any or lease payment escalation, if any;
(iii) security deposit extended to the RESCO as part of the PPA or lease agreement, if any;
(iv) O&M cost per period to be paid to the RESCO as agreed separately in the PPA or lease agreement, if any (typically included in PPA price or lease payment); and
(v) replacement cost of spare parts per period as agreed separately in the PPA or lease agreement, if any (typically included in PPA price or lease payment).

Cash Inflows (in case of existing power source = grid)

(i) current price per unit (kWh) of electricity consumed from the grid, including peak/off-peak consumption tariffs and average consumption in kWh at each of these tariff categories;

(ii) monthly/annual fixed charges based on connected load, if any;

(iii) grid usage and other charges, if any;

(iv) average expected increase in price per unit (kWh) of electricity, based on historical averages and market-based projections; and

(v) other charges, taxes and levies in connection to maintenance of the grid connection, if any.

2.4 Economic or Cost–Benefit Analysis

Economic analysis refers to analysis of costs and benefits flowing to and from the broader economy. This could mean (depending on the project context) quantifying nonmarket and/or non-cashflow benefits, internalization of externalities, and/or accounting for subsidies. Economic analysis generally includes the following:

(i) quantifiable economic benefits that would typically include cashflow and non-cashflow benefits; for example, an on-grid microgrid installation would typically reduce electricity costs of the consumer (direct cashflow benefits), but may also create additional jobs locally and/or reduce carbon emissions (indirect non-cashflow benefits);

(ii) the economic net present value of the project as well as economic internal rate of return; and

(iii) the outcome of the sensitivity analysis.

While financial analysis includes the cost of the project as paid by the project developer and the benefits of the project to the project developer (as revenues or cost saving), economic analysis includes costs and benefits of the project to the broader economy or society (and not just to the project developer or consumer).

Economic analysis could use nominal or real prices provided that the discount rate is consistent with the choice made.

2.5 Microgrid Policies and Regulations in Asia

Microgrid policies and regulations vary across Asia, and some countries, such as Japan, the PRC, and Thailand have supportive policies and/or pilot programs for urban and industrial microgrids whereas others have yet to introduce such policies. Several countries such as Bangladesh, Cambodia, India, Indonesia, Maldives, Myanmar, Nepal, and the Philippines have developed and implemented off-grid minigrid policies for increasing access to energy. Including grid-connected or off-grid microgrids as a policy within a country's power or energy system needs to be a strategic decision-making process (Figure 35).[14]

Some of the key policy and regulatory enablers for urban and industrial microgirds are:

(i) **Specific urban and industrial microgrid policy.** A specially defined policy for urban and industrial microgrids would help facilitate private and public sector investments, as well as provide stability for such microgrid. This policy should clearly define the goals of deploying urban and industrial microgrids, provide technical specifications and standards, identify eligible consumers, determine grid interconnection norms, tariffs, and licensing and documentation requirements. So far, only developed countries such as Japan and the Republic of Korea, and upper middle-income countries such as the PRC

---

[14] Source: EUEI-PDF, Alliance for Rural Electrification (ARE), EU/RECP and REN21 mini-grid policy toolkit (2014).

Figure 35: Strategic Process for Microgrids

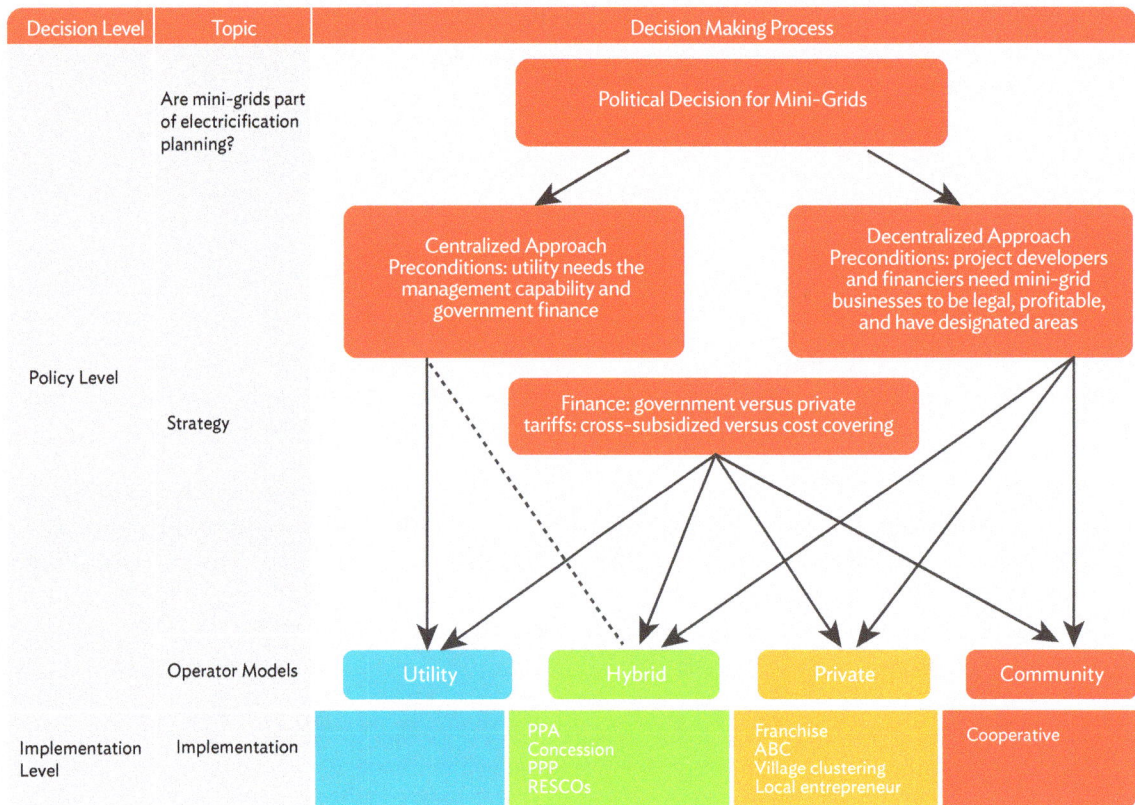

ABC = anchor business community, PPA = power purchase agreement, PPP = public–private partnership, RESCO = renewable energy service company.

Source: Allesi, P. L. (n.d.) *Universal Access To Energy and the Role Of Regulation.* https://turinschool.eu/files/ turinschool/ISS16_ Alessi.pdf.

and Thailand have defined such policies or programs in Asia. Other developed countries such as the US and a few European countries have also defined such policies and programs.

(ii)   **Net metering or gross metering policies.** Net metering or gross metering policies enable microgrids to be connected to the national grid and export excess electricity to the grid. Such policies enable urban and industrial renewable energy-based microgrids to use the grid instead of the expensive battery or energy storage solutions, to increase their autonomy. This will also improve their economics by supplying excess electricity to the grid for economic considerations (net or gross metered). While net or gross metering for stand-alone, single customer rooftop, or ground-mounted solar installations are available in many developed and developing countries in Asia, these have not yet been defined for microgrids in most countries.

(iii) **Technical standards and specifications for grid interconnection.** This would allow microgrids to design and plan according to specified technical standards and hence, manage grid interconnection technical design and costs more reasonably. While grid interconnection norms for stand-alone, single customer rooftop, or ground-mounted solar installations are available in many developed and developing countries in Asia, these have not yet been defined for microgrids in most countries.

(iv)   **Open access or contestable consumer model.** Open access policies and regulations allow electricity consumers—typically only large C&I consumers (known as contestable consumers) —to choose their electricity service provider, rather than being confined to purchasing electricity from a government-owned or private monopoly utility. Such contestable consumers are often served by open access developers or merchant power plants that develop and install these assets either remotely or locally, as onsite rooftop solar or microgrid installations and using national grid T&D infrastructure to supply electricity. Countries such as India, the PRC, the Philippines, and Singapore have such regulations in place, whereas countries such as Viet Nam are in the process of introducing similar policies. Nevertheless, treatment of open access and/or contestable consumers by onsite microgrids is still not defined in most countries of Asia, and such clarity would enable more microgrid investments.

(v) **Simpler electricity generation and distribution licensing.** In many countries, electricity generation and distribution is still a highly regulated and licensed activity and requires complex documentation and approval process for microgrid developers to obtain such licenses. Simplifying these regulations would increase developers' interest in setting up microgrids.

(vi) **Feed-in-tariffs and other financial incentives.** Tariff support and other financial incentives such as subsidies and tax benefits for microgrids would enable developers to deploy microgrids even for consumers where financial viability without such incentives is a barrier.

(vii) **Risk-sharing mechanisms for debt financing.** Considering the limited understanding and interest from commercial banks and lenders in many developing countries to finance microgrids, any risk-sharing mechanisms, such as credit guarantees or blended finance structures, could help microgrid developers raise debt finance at affordable interest rates.

Financing models typically follow local policies and regulations (Table 9).

Table 9: Financing Models for Microgrids

Structure	Description and Examples

Financed entirely or largely by grants (capital subsidies) – typically for pilot and/or demonstration urban, industrial, island microgrid installations or off-grid energy access focused minigrid installations	• Typically for pilot and/or demonstration urban microgrids or off-grid community-minigrids
	• Examples:
	  ° New Energy and Industrial Technology Development Organization (NEDO) Microgrids Program in Japan
	  ° The World Bank and the Government of Myanmar Minigrid Program for increasing access to energy in Myanmar (with implementation support from the GIZ)

Financed by a suitable debt–equity–grant ratio
Grant used for capital subsidies
	• Typically for RESCO or IPP-owned models
	• Grant level might be fixed or provided as viability gap funding
	• Examples:
	  ° Some state-level urban microgrid programs in the United States
	  ° Rockefeller Foundation's Smart Power for Rural Development Program in India and Myanmar

Financed by a suitable debt–equity ratio but with operating expense subsidies (concessional tariffs to consumers)	• Typically for utility-owned models
	• Many times includes concessional debt
	• Examples:
	  ° Minigrid installations by rural electric cooperatives (utilities) or qualified third parties in the Philippines
	  ° Some microgrid installations in Europe

GIZ = Deutsche Gesellschaft für Internationale Zusammenarbeit, IPP = independent power producer, RESCO = renewable energy service company.
Source: ADB.

Financing of microgrids in most countries go through the transition depicted in Table 10 wherein they start with mainly grant or subsidy-based financing and gradually move toward commercial investments as business models and financial viability are established.

Table 10: Microgrid Subsidies

Fully-Subsidized	**Partially-Subsidized**	**For Profit**
> Costs are fully subsidized by government and/or donors > In-kind contributions from the community are common > Cost recovery tariffs nominally cover some O&M and admin expenses, but often do not end up being collected over time	> Large subsidies for capital costs > O&M cost recovery occurs from tariff	> No subsidies > O&M cost recovered by tariff collection > Tariffs provide a return on the nonsubsidized portion of the capital cost

O&M = operation and maintenance.
Source: Energy4Impact (previously known as GVEP International). 2014. *Financing Mini-Grids in East Africa*. https://www.german-energy-solutions.de/GES/Redaktion/DE/Publikationen/ Praesentationen/2015/2015-03-19-iv-mini-grids-03-gvep.pdf?__blob=publicationFile&v=9.

The financial viability of microgrids is subject to a number of risks and mitigating these risks with suitable measures is important to ensure bankability. Some of these risks and possible mitigating measures are described in Table 11 .

Table 11: Challenges and Risks in the Implementation of Microgrids

Risks	Mitigation Measures
Grid Electrification Risks (Business Risk) – applicable only to off-grid and remote microgrids	• Develop minigrids in locations not too close to the main grid • A government minigrid policy that provides grid integration and exit options to RESCOs and IPPs when grid arrives • Include grid integration elements into system design • Work closely with government and/or utilities on-grid electrification plans • Sign agreements with government and/or utility that a PPA will be signed with the utility (at Feed-in-Tariff [FiT], if possible) when grid arrives
Consumer Payment Risks (Credit Risk)	• Develop a robust consumer credit risk appraisal system – to be conducted as part of up-front site appraisal and/or selection process • Conduct consumer income and/or energy expense surveys, use credit history from microfinance institutions • Prepaid or pay-as-you-go metering solutions

continued on next page

Table 11 *continued*

Risks	Mitigation Measures
Technology and Product Risk	• Built into system design, so that system is modular and components can be replaced later • Constantly monitor technology and market development • Supplier and/or manufacturer warranties to protect against product failure
Capacity Utilization Risk (Lower than Estimated Uptake of Electricity from customers)	• Load estimation done rigorously at the time of site surveys and/or selection • Actively develop productive uses of energy (PUE) measures to increase off-take and economic activities that could reduce payment risks (in case of remote, off-grid minigrids); strategies for managing seasonality of load • Grid integration
Regulatory Risk	• Constant dialogue with government and/or regulators • Involve bilateral and/or multilateral agencies in a policy dialogue with government
Operational Risk	• Robust internal operational systems • Training and internal audits • Legal and compliance

IPPs = independent power producers, PPA = power purchase agreement, RESCO = renewable energy service company.
Source: ADB.

Nevertheless, many of these technology, regulatory, and business risks manifest into barriers to achieving bankability and financial close of microgrid projects (Figure 36).

Figure 36: Barriers to Financing

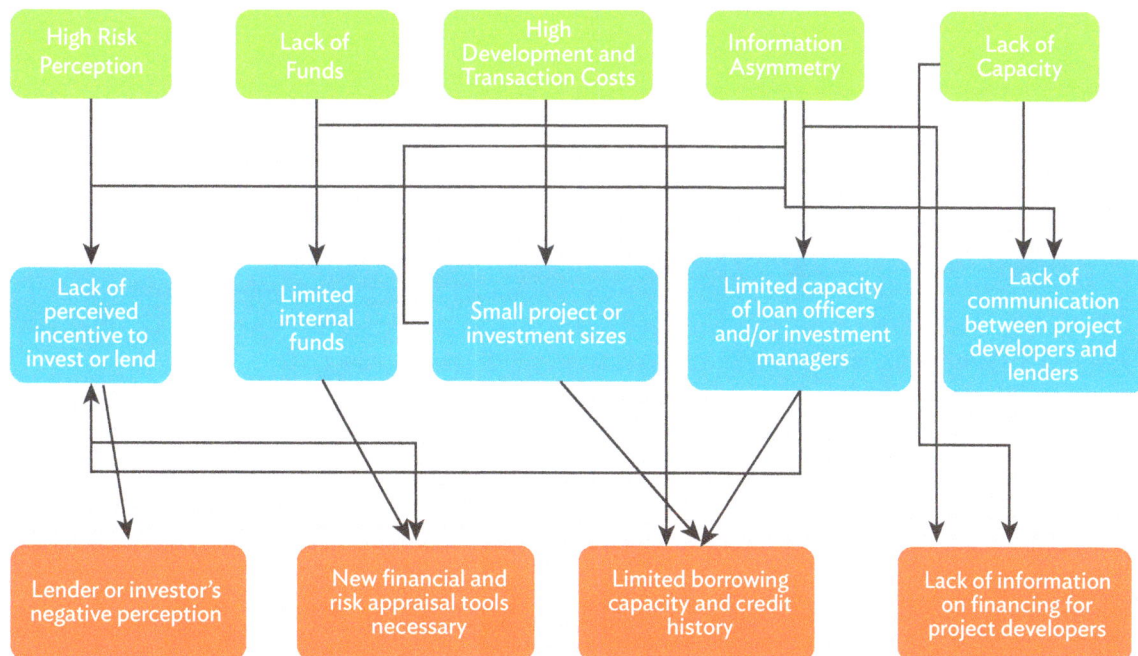

Source: Souche, A. 2014. *Financing of Clean Energy Projects in Southeast Asia: Challenges and Opportunities*. Renewable Energy World Asia 2014. https://www.dfdl.com/wp-content/uploads/2014/10/dfdl%20financing%20 of%20clean%20energy%20 projects%20in%20south%20east%20asia%20%20challenges%20and%20 opportunities.pdf.

Both project developers and lenders can develop several measures to reduce financial viability and bankability concerns and risks of financing microgrids. Some of them are described in Table 12.

Table 12: Measures for Making Microgrids Bankable for Both Project Developers and Lenders or Investors

Project Developer's Side	Lender or Investor's Side
Customer Credit Appraisal Systems	
Smart or mobile phone-based payment systems	Concessional credit lines from development banks
Customer repayment data and predictive analytics	Better understanding of risks
First-loss guarantees for off-balance sheet financing	Better understanding of risks
Robust product development, sales, distribution, supply chain and after-sales service systems	Improved risk appraisal tools
Strong CXOs, especially CFOs	Loan or invesment officer training

CFO = chief financial officer, CXO = chief x officer.
Source: ADB.

Capacity Building

Many DMCs, ministries, government agencies, and utilities in Asia that develop, promulgate, and implement microgrid policies tend to lack the necessary technical knowledge and trained staff. Government-owned utilities, project developers, and IPPs also lack the technical capacity required to identify suitable locations for microgrid projects, conduct detailed feasibility studies, and develop detailed project reports (DPRs) that are bankable. Many of these project developers are new to the microgrid or renewable energy sector and lack the capability to complete the required feasibility studies; find sufficient financing; and implement, operate, and maintain projects. Additionally, there is limited or no access to startup capital that is required to finance feasibility studies and develop DPRs. There is a lack of local capacity—technical experts, equipment suppliers, and EPC contractors—for microgrid project development and deployment in many of these countries.

Knowledge management and capacity building activities are an important area of support for DMCs in Asia on microgrids. Although developing countries in Asia have started to take the lead in urban and industrial microgrids at scale, this is limited to few countries such as Japan, the Republic of Korea, the PRC, and Thailand. There is a clear gap in understanding the factors that influence the success or failure during the process of developing bankable projects in developing countries of Asia. Developing knowledge products such as handbooks, and toolkits, and organizing a series of workshops, roadshows, and investment fora to disseminate the policymaking, project development, and implementation experience among DMCs is necessary to increase the deployment of microgrids in Asia.

Microgrid-related technical, operational, and other skills development within ADB member countries is also an important activity, given the lack of trained personnel for project implementation. Skills development is required at different levels and skill requirements vary depending on the type of projects. For example, deploying grid-connected microgrids requires different skills than designing large solar parks. Needs and current skill levels in DMCs have to be considered before designing and deploying training and capacity building activities.

Box 3: Demonstration and Deployment Case 3

Case Study: Dawanshan Island Microgrid in the People's Republic of China

Location	Dawanshan Island, Southeast of Guangdong
Country	The People's Republic of China
Year of Commissioning	2011
Asset Owner and Sponsor	State Grid Corporation of China
Asset Developer	Singyes Solar
Microgrid Technology	Wind Generators 1×850 kW
	PV Arrays 200 kWp
	Lead-Acid Battery 2,000 kWh
	PCS 1,000 kW
	Diesel Generators 2×500 kW
Business Model	Up-front capital Investment by local utility or government agency
Grid Connection	Island grid
Capital Expenditure	$2.78 million
Installation Type	Capital investment by utility or state-funded
Total Electricity Generated per Annum	~2.68 million kWh per annum
Simple Payback Period	More than 25 years

kW = kilowatt, kWh = kilowatt-hour, PV = photovoltaic.

Project Background

Formerly known as the Ladrones Islands, the Wanshan Archipelago is a 104-island archipelago that is part of the Xiangzhou District of Zhuhai in Guangdong Province, PRC. Wanshan Archipelago is a prominent tourist vacation spot. Da Wanshan island is a part of Wanshan Archipelago. At the time that this microgrid was conceived, the population of the island was 300 and its land area is 8.1 km^2. Main industries on the island are fishing and tourism.

Da Wanshan's main source of power supply was diesel generators that cost ~$0.56 (CNY~3.5) per kWh as compared to the cost of grid electricity of $0.07 (CNY 0.5) per unit in Guangdong Province. Diesel power on the island also had low reliability. Load demand was seasonal, with high demand from May to October (tourism season) and low demand in November to April periods. Peak load on the island was 810 kW with 59% of load between 200 kW to 400 kW.

Key Considerations

(i)   The PRC's National Smart Grid Project wanted to set up demonstration microgrids based on renewable energy to assess their suitability for island populations. Renewable energy-powered microgrids were considered for their economic feasibility and environmental friendliness.

(ii)   Increasing demand for power supply by residents of the island with its growing attraction in the tourism circuit required increased reliability of electricity.

(iii)   Under the National Grid Project model, the government also wanted to explore new energy-utilization models backed by sound financial or economic incentives that can be later replicated to other areas with similar needs and requirements.

continued on next page

Box 3 *continued*

Project Description

The Wanshan Island New Energy Microgrid Demonstration Project was set up under the National Key Smart Grid Project, with an aim to build the smart microgrid for Guishan Island, Dong'ao Island, and Dawanshan Island. The microgrid setup at Da Wanshan island consisted of one wind generator with 850 kW capacity, solar PV arrays with 200 kWp capacity, lead-acid battery with 2,000 kWh capacity, power conditioning system with 1,000 kW, and two diesel generators with 500 kW capacity each.

Business Model and Commercial Details

Da Wanshan island microgrid was set up by State Grid Corporation of the PRC with Singyes Solar as the main EPC contractor. The microgrid was set up with a capital expenditure of $2.78 million.

As the payback period for the project is more than 25 years, subsidies from the government are needed to make this project commercially viable. Based on a case study,[a] this microgrid would be commercially viable under one of the two scenarios:

(i) A capital subsidy of the amount of 70% of initial investment, which would result in payback period of 8.15 years.

(ii) An operational subsidy of $0.065 per kWh of electricity for 10 years, which would result in a payback period of 8.31 years.

Sources: Honghua, X. 2015. *Status and Challenges of Micro-Grid Demonstration in China*. https://events.development.asia/system/files/materials/2015/05/201505-status-and-challenges-microgrid-demonstration-china.pdf, and Wanshan Archipelago. The Wanshan Archipelago: Wikipedia. https://en.wikipedia.org/wiki/Wanshan_Archipelago.

---

[a] Professor Wang from Tinajin University, PRC. https://microgrid-symposiums.org/wp-content/uploads/2014/12/tianjin_chengshan-wang.pdf.

Box 4: Demonstration and Deployment Case 4

Case Study: 500 kW Microgrid at Nagoya Landfill, Japan

Location	Nagoya Landfill
Country	Japan
Year of Commissioning	2014
Asset Owner or Sponsor	Local landfill owners
Utility	Chubu Electric Power Company, Inc.
Developer and/or Vendor(s)	Optimal Power Solutions
Renewable Energy Technology	Solar PV and Energy Storage System
Renewable Energy Installation Size	500 KW
Business Model	Feed-in-tariff (FiT)
Grid Connection	Grid-connected
Energy Storage System	0.2 MW/1.2 MWh lead-acid battery bank
Total Cost of the Project	~$1.5 million
Installation Model	FiT model
Simple Payback Period	~4 years

MW = megawatt, PV = photovoltaic.

Project Description

The Nagoya landfill microgrid facility is a 500 kW solar power generation unit located at Nagoya in Japan. The microgrid installation is backed up by a 200 KW battery storage system. The microgrid was considered and constructed to increase the value proposition of the property for landfill owners. The leading developer for this project was Optimal Power Solutions of Australia. Due to their low cost at that time, lead-acid batteries were chosen, but the project investors envision to replace the battery bank at the end of their life or after approximately 6 years of initial commissioning, with lithium-ion batteries, given their rapidly falling prices.

With its battery based long-duration dispatch of solar PV energy, this microgrid provides firm capacity to the grid during peak demand periods, and in case of a grid outage, it also offers a resilient power source to local loads. As the local utility feeders are saturated with solar PV, the value that additional solar PV can bring in the late morning and early afternoon was limited. At the same time, since there is a strong impetus in Japan to reduce reliance on imported fossil fuels and to phase out large centralized nuclear power plants, distributed solar PV is a top priority for utilities and regulators. In such a situation, a special FiT was agreed for installations such as these. Import of electricity from grid is not allowed. Therefore, a one-directional inverter has been installed. During the peak net load period, typically between 4 p.m. and 9 p.m. and sometimes as late as 2 a.m., the battery bank discharges to supply electricity to the grid. The battery bank is rated for 6 hours. However, sometimes it also discharges for 8 hours to 10 hours.

Navigating through the intricacies of Japanese utility interconnection requirements was one of the biggest challenges for the developer given the nature of DER and their high occurrence in the Japanese grid.

continued on next page

Box 4 *continued*

Key Considerations

(i)   As described in the *Microgrid Analysis and Case Studies Report* by California Energy Commission, the 2-acre host site is a landfill. In this case, the site is paved with about 6 feet of soil under it. As most types of construction were not possible on such a site, a microgrid installation was the most appropriate and opportunistic use of this land.

(ii) Within a tightly regulated electricity market, the utilities and regulators in Japan are in a contrasting situation where they have to reduce dependence on fossil fuels and nuclear power plants on one hand and encourage take-up of renewable energy on the other. However, given the intermittent nature of renewable energy it is difficult to integrate renewable energy power assets into the grid. With Nagoya Microgrid fulfilling both the needs of the utility, to have renewable energy and peak demand capacity through battery discharge, the project was commissioned with special FiT.

Business Model and Commercial Details

Approximately 10% of the funding for the project was made by the primary project sponsor. A third party financed the remainder in lieu of routine payments over the 15-year lifetime of the project. A challenge faced during financing was that FiT is not fixed and can vary with time. Special tariffs paid by the utility is the primary revenue stream for this project. Simple payback for this project is estimated to be around 4 years.

Source: California Energy Commission. 2018. *Microgrid Analysis and Case Studies Report*.
https://ww2.energy.ca.gov/2018publications/CEC-500-2018-022/CEC-500-2018-022.pdf.

3 Future Development

3.1 Role of Microgrids in the Electricity Ecosystem of the Future

3.1.1 Decarbonization, Digitalization, Decentralization, and Non-Wires Solutions

Decarbonization, Digitalization, Decentralization (collectively often referred to as 3D) has become the buzzword approach to next generation electricity networks. While a century ago, centralized electricity production made huge progress in economy and civilization possible, including improved economies of scale and power plant efficiency, in the current scenario, it is 3D that could help address today's energy challenges including an optimized way to access reliable, resilient, clean energy (Figure 37). An important approach within this framework is microgrids, especially smart and connected microgrids that create a locally and/or regionally interconnected energy system incorporating DERs, loads, storage, control, and energy management. Consequently, several studies and expert opinions point to microgrids as the technically feasible solution to contribute to the energy transition. Microgrids provide an accessible practical pathway in improving energy accessibility, independence, supply reliability and resiliency, flexibility, and cost optimization. They have the ability to participate in grid balancing DR incentive programs and expanding the adoption of intermittent renewable clean generation like solar PV and wind. Technical advances in the microgrids core constituent technologies (Section 1), especially monitoring and communications, have been key to making this possible.

A non-wire solution (NWS) is an alternative approach to electricity ecosystem evolution, which is fundamentally aligned to the 3D philosophy. Navigant (2017) describes NWS as: "An electric grid project or infrastructure investment using nontraditional T&D solutions, such as DG, DER, energy storage, DSM, DR, energy efficiency, microgrids, and grid software and controls, to defer or replace the need for specific equipment upgrades, such as new transmission lines or transformers, by reducing the load at substation or circuit level."

Traditionally, when a regulated utility needs to replace or upgrade T&D infrastructure, new equipment would be procured and installed, and the regulators would adjust the electricity pricing to allow the utility to earn a fair rate of return on the new infrastructural investment. Usually, other alternatives were not examined, and it was considered equipment upgrade or replacement expenditure, part of the cost of doing business. However, as grid management and DER technologies advance, the same drivers as for microgrids (affordability, reliability, and environmental benefits, as described in Section 1 of this handbook) are resulting in nontraditional solutions such as NWS (of which microgrids themselves are an important component) being explored to achieve the required T&D objectives.

As a flip side to the position taken in this subsection, and as we will see in the next subsection 3.1.2, while 3D and NWS (including microgrids) hold an important place in the electricity ecosystem of the future, conventional T&D capacity will still play a role. Essentially, costs, time, and functionality in implementing 3D or NWS need to be initially assessed, and compared to conventional T&D. While in many instances 3D or NWD will win, it is a key analysis toward balancing the consideration of centralized versus decentralized in fulfilling a utility's mandate to provide affordable, reliable, and safe service to its customers.

Figure 37: Evolution of the Electricity Grid

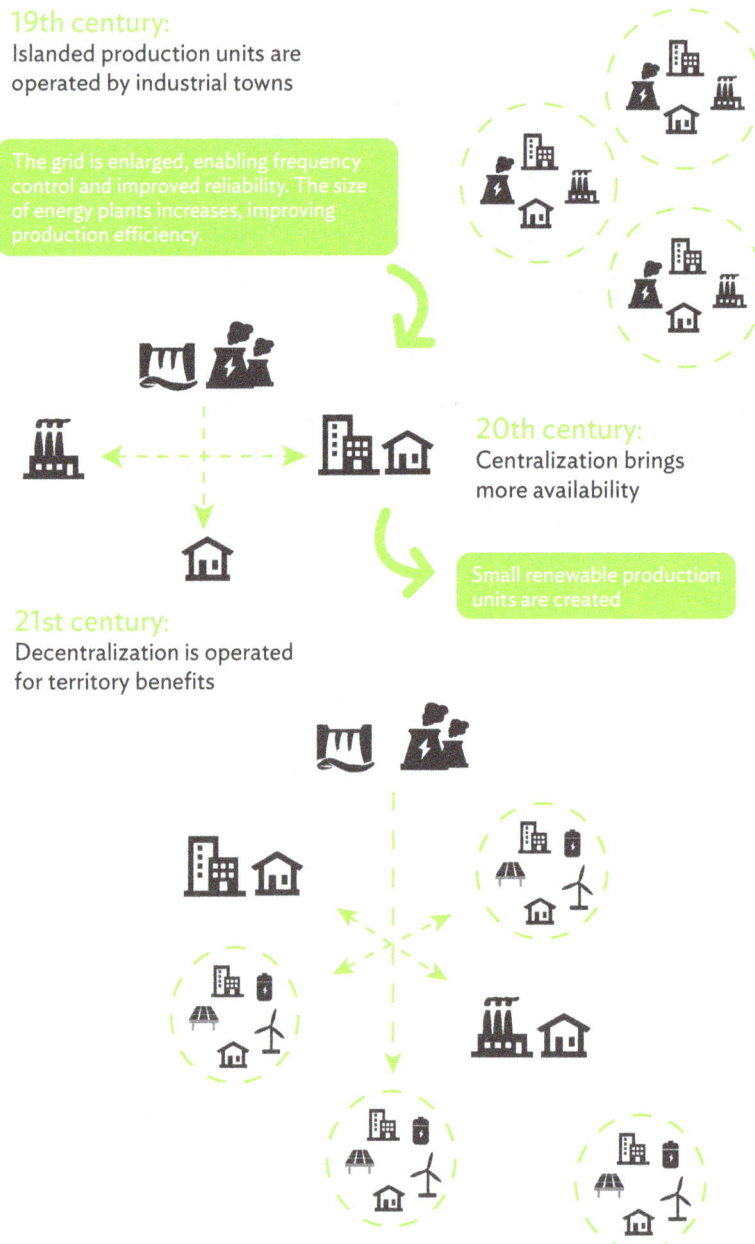

19th century:
Islanded production units are operated by industrial towns

The grid is enlarged, enabling frequency control and improved reliability. The size of energy plants increases, improving production efficiency.

20th century:
Centralization brings more availability

Small renewable production units are created

21st century:
Decentralization is operated for territory benefits

Source: Schneider Electric. 2016. *How Microgrids Contribute to the Energy Transition*. https://sun-connect-news.org/ fileadmin/ DATEIEN/Dateien/New/9982095_12-01-16A_EN.pdf.

3.1.2 The Flip Side: A Case for Continued Addition of Transmission Capacity

It has been argued in some quarters that due to minigrids and microgrids, new transmission grid investments have become less important. This may be relevant only for the specific context of rural minigrids. As a holistic strategy, if the intent is to increase the level of renewable energy penetration in the grid, then adding transmission capacity also has a key role to play to complement grid edge investments in distribution networks and microgrids. If we consider a high level of renewables penetration (which are almost always intermittent if excluding hydropower) to be the backbone of our electricity system, the following points become pertinent:

(i)   Good solar resource and good wind resource are often at different locations, so while they complement each other in terms of time of day, that electricity still needs to be transported over long distances. This needs adequate transmission capacity, and when the transmission is intercountry, the role of regional cooperation and integration becomes important.

(ii)   To generate electricity from renewables requires a lot of land. This land tends to be farther away from the population centers and load centers. On the other hand, urban areas having large demand lack the land for renewables or the land is prohibitively expensive. This scenario also requires a grid to transmit power over longer distances. For example, solar PV panels on every single US rooftop would provide only 40% of the total power requirement. A target like 90% renewables would still need doubling of the current transmission capacity (Schneider Electric 2016). Proof of this is that Texas has become the largest wind power state in the US by building transmission to evacuate the renewable power. In addition, although solar power can be quite modular and distributed, other renewables (e.g., wind, offshore wind, geothermal, hydro) are more cost-effective at scale. As such, there will be a need for transmission of larger power generation sources to load centers. This is why distribution level investments alone may not be enough for the future scenario, rather it needs to be a mix of more transmission capacity in conjunction with grid edge investments like microgrids.

(iii) If we target electrifying the transport sector, additional transmission would be needed. For example, Tesla super charger for trucks is rated at 2 MW, which needs electricity in the magnitudes described above—even more so if the building heating and district heating sectors were considered by an extension of this logic.

(iv)   According to a recent study (Brattle Group 2019),[15] an additional $30 billion to $90 billion of additional transmission would be needed by 2030 in the US alone (20%–50% over the past 10 years' levels), and $200 billion to $600 billion by 2050 (50% to 170% increase over the current levels). Transmission line approvals, land acquisition, and financial closure (payback model) are complicated, so transmission projects face the risk of getting delayed. Another disadvantage is the "single point of failure" type loss of resilience when fault in large transmission line. Undergrounding reduces some of the problems of transmission line fault, but is much more expensive.

Thus, 3D and microgrids should be considered a complementary building block, rather than disruptive, to the centralized grid in developing countries as well.

3.1.3 Microgrids: Key Relevance to the Transportation Sector

Apart from the electricity supply sector itself, the EV transportation ecosystem is a foundational sector that deserves specific highlight, as this is an area where microgrids have an enormous ability to help transform. This is partly because of the sheer size of the sector. Worldwide, transportation as a whole consumes over 30% of primary energy, and electrifying only a small percentage of this in the coming years would translate to a lot of capacity. To ensure adequate energy, this new charging infrastructure will have to be installed on the utility grid in

---

[15]   While Brattle Group is an industry group, NREL also came to a similar conclusion.

combination with grid edge technologies, like DERs and energy storage. But sometimes, utility support might not be possible, and in such cases microgrid infrastructure can fill the gap to enable charging stations to cater to the charging demand. In addition, a decentralized infrastructure will allow the many actors in the EV ecosystem to capitalize on the flexibility of EVs. One promising way to do this being "vehicle-to-grid" (V2G), wherein EVs can sell DR services to the power grid, either by throttling their charging rate or even returning power to the grid.

One of the fundamental impediments to growth of the EV ecosystem is the lack of better aligned business models and pricing structure associated with the sale of energy. This results in the paucity of readily available charging stations. The current EV charging infrastructure is as "dirty" as the local utility grid is, and new energy solutions, including renewable energy, energy storage and microgrids, if integrated, can enable a more robust, widespread, and cleaner EV charging infrastructure.

In summary, the reliable EV charging infrastructure that microgrids can enable is something that needs to be widespread and readily available, to truly enable a vibrant EV ecosystem. In addition to workplaces and communities, EV charging stations will need to be developed in three key types of locations: at destination points, along highways, and near public transportation nodes like airports, and bus and train stations.

3.1.4 Relevance of Microgrids to the Current Power System Situation in ADB Developing Member Countries

The current power system situation, in terms of both technology level and regulations wise, varies significantly across ADB DMCs. In general, power consuming end users in developing countries typically do not have access to high-quality reliable power and have to contend with frequent power outages, in contrast to their counterparts in developed countries. Developing countries also often have weak grid infrastructures due to underinvesment and poor management, leading to high power losses and theft, thereby hindering the success of business and industry and depriving people of a better quality of life. This is the value proposition for grid-connected microgrids in developing countries, and the reason why the indirect costs of the status quo outweigh the huge initial investment required to change it. Furthermore, grid-connected microgrids are the building blocks of smart grids and smart supergrids, which have the potential to help developing countries leapfrog, by revolutionalizing the power sector, similar to what the internet did to information.

For the above reasons and to address one or more of the various drivers described in Section 1, grid-connected microgrids are well suited for deployment in practically all the ADB DMCs. Microgrid applicability in selected ADB DMCs is summarized in Table 13, and selected microgrids in ASEAN are shown in Figure 38.

**Table 13: Power Situation and Microgrid Drivers in Selected
ADB Developing Member Countries**

DMC	Power Situation	Key Microgrid Drivers
Bangladesh	• Low installed generation capacity (20 GW in 2019 mostly natural gas), and low per capita consumption • Problems include poor transmission and distribution infrastructure high system losses, low plant efficiency, electricity theft • Low renewable energy generation (<20 MW) currently, but moderately high potential of 3.6 GW	• Affordable electricity from DG • Environmental benefits of DG to supplement utility scale renewable energy • Overall reliability and resilience in the face of inadequate T&D infrastructure
India	• Third largest producer and consumer of electricity in world but low per capita consumption • Surplus generation capacity (365 GW in 2019) but low capacity factor and inadequate distribution infrastructure • 55% coal; 12% hydro; 10% solar; 12% wind (2019) • Ambitious target to increase renewable energy from 80 GW in 2019 to 175 GW by 2022	• Affordable electricity from microgrids with DG in remote or rural areas • Reliability and resilience in the face of inadequate distribution infrastructure for remote or rural and C&I customers
Myanmar	• Low installed capacity (5 GW); low per capita • Limited grid coverage • 75% hydro, 20% NG; Good potential for renewable energy	• Affordable electricity from DG as poor grid coverage • Reliability and resilience for C&I and grid stability
Nepal	• 23% electricity is imported. Remaining is mostly run of river hydro (1 GW) • No known fossil fuel reserves, but large 44 GW potential from hydro • Low per capita electricity consumption • Limited T&D infrastructure	• Affordable electricity from DG as poor grid coverage • Reliability and resilience for C&I and grid stability • DG in rural or remote weak grid and off-grid areas
Philippines	• 20 GW installed with moderately low per capita • Restructuring has resulted in heavy cost burden to government and consumers • 43% coal; 24% NG; 12% hydro; 13% geothermal; <0.5% solar, wind, and biomass (scope to increase)	• Affordable electricity from DG as load centers are far from generation location • DG in remote islands weak grid and off-grid areas • Reliability and resilience for C&I
Thailand	• 90% of electricity is thermal generation (60% NG, 25% coal) • Thailand+GMS can achieve 100% renewable energy (mostly via hydro) by 2050	• Environmental friendly renewable energy DG to supplement the mostly thermal utility generators • Reliability and resilience for C&I

C&I = commercial and industrial, DG = distributed generators, DMC = developing member country, GW = gigawatt, MW = megawatt, T&D = transmission and distribution.

Figure 38: Selected Microgrids in Association of Southeast Asian Nations

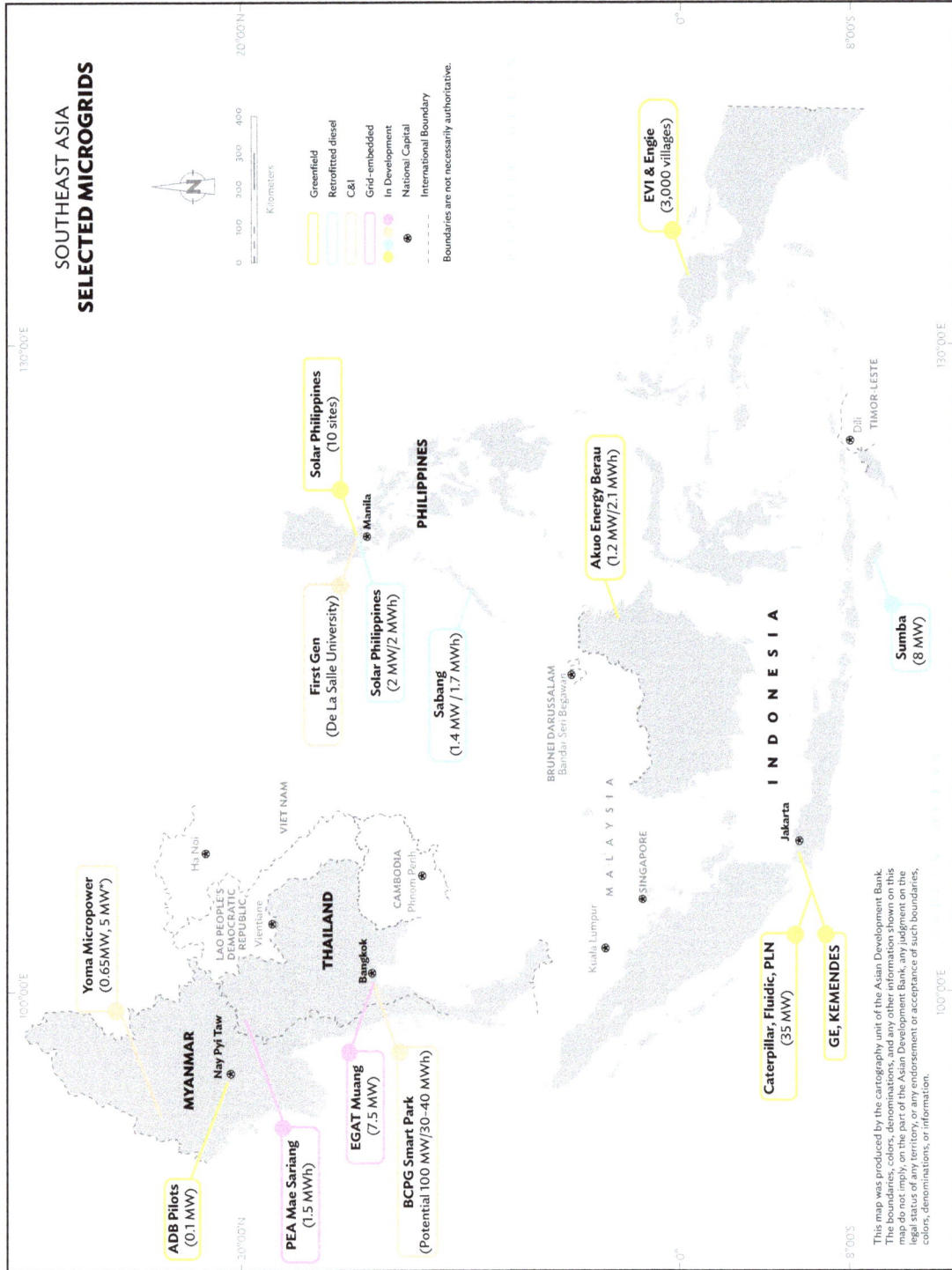

MW = megawatt.

Source: Kawahara, T., ed. 2019. *Distributed Renewable Energy in Emerging Countries*. ADB workshop papers. Tokyo: Bloomberg New Energy Finance.

South Asia in particular suffers from the double problems of having the second largest population in the world that is off-grid (next to only Sub-Saharan Africa) and the low quality of supply (i.e., power cuts and unreliable power). This has resulted in the per capita electricity consumption being the second-lowest in the world. At 707 kWh, it is less than one-quarter of the world average, with only Sub-Saharan Africa being lower. This has a major detrimental impact on economic development. For instance, if all of India's population were to be connected to the grid with access to 24/7 reliable electricity, the income of rural households could increase by $9.4 billion a year, and eliminating power cuts can prevent about $22.7 billion in business losses (Zhang 2019).

The number of electrical outages a month and frequency of these outages are even worse in South Asia than in Sub-Saharan Africa (Figure 39), although this is likely due to far lower grid connectivity in Sub-Saharan Africa.

Figure 39: Power Supply Reliability by Region

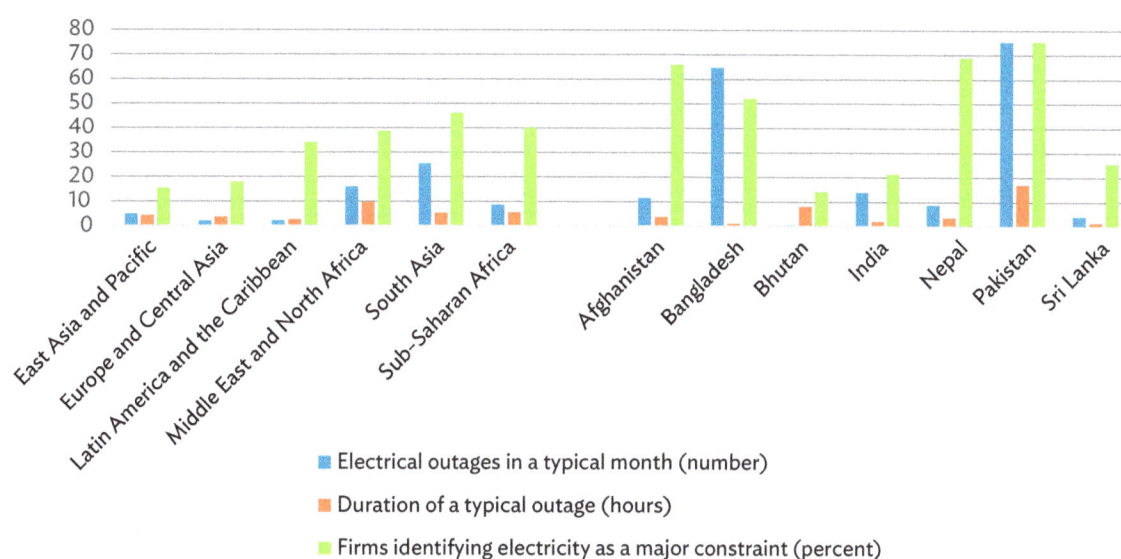

- Electrical outages in a typical month (number)
- Duration of a typical outage (hours)
- Firms identifying electricity as a major constraint (percent)

Source: World Bank Enterprise Surveys in Afghanistan (2014), Bangladesh (2013), Bhutan (2015), India (2014), Nepal (2013), Pakistan (2014), and Sri Lanka (2011).

3.1.5 Approaches to Promote Grid-Connected Microgrids and Replicate Pilots

From a technology and application perspective, as ADB DMCs develop from low-income to middle-income countries, the drivers for microgrids will begin to align with what is being seen in developed countries. Consequently, many of the drivers for microgrids in ADB DMCs (Table 13), are similar to the motivations for operational microgrids in the US (Figure 40). This line of thought should guide the replication of microgrid pilots in DMCs. Overall benefits can be maximized with the adoption of a high-level architecture that involves a "federation of microgrids" each solving the best they can, the needs of their own localized off-takers, but sharing and harmonizing what they can in a centralized fashion throughout the grid, which is often emerging or weak.

From a policy and regulatory standpoint, governments and policy makers in ADB DMCs should aim to include microgrids (both on-grid and off-grid) in their power system planning and design. Specific policies and regulations to clarify microgrid as a distinct power asset class and their technical standards in terms of grid interconnection will go a long way in incentivizing microgrid investments. Pilot and demonstration microgrids have been installed in nearly all ADB DMCs, although most of them are off-grid, energy access focused. Only a few countries such as Japan, the Republic of Korea, and the PRC have installed several pilot and/or demonstration microgrids, and the installation of more of these systems in ADB DMCs, funded by government and/or development capital, could also play an important role in demonstrating the role of microgrids in future power systems of ADB DMCs. Clarity on tariffs, licensing, and permitting for microgrids would also be beneficial, while targeted concessional lines of credit and financial risk-sharing facilities from development financial institutions such as ADB would help increase access to finance to microgrids in ADB DMCs.

Figure 40: Three Primary Motivations for Operational Microgrids in the United States

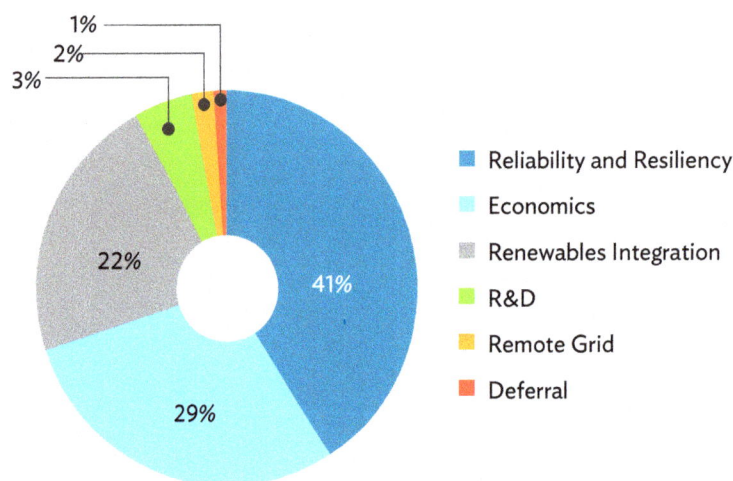

Legend:
- Reliability and Resiliency
- Economics
- Renewables Integration
- R&D
- Remote Grid
- Deferral

Values shown: 41%, 29%, 22%, 3%, 2%, 1%

R&D = research and development.
Source: Wood MacKenzie Power and Renewables. 2019. *Microgrid Market Overview.* https://www.greentechmedia.com/webinars/webinar/at-the-edge-of-the-grid-best-practices-in-utility-digitalization-and-busine.

Apart from this handbook and additional resources available online, ADB has also published other reports and guidebooks relevant to the origination, structuring, execution, and deployment of grid-connected microgrids in DMCs. While many of these were written with a minigrids focus, they are of definite relevance to microgrids as well. They include:

1. *Handbook on Battery Energy Storage System* (ADB 2018)

2. *Developing Renewable Energy Mini-Grids in Myanmar* (ADB 2017)

3. *Deployment of Hybrid Renewable Energy Systems in Minigrids* (ADB 2017)

4. *Guidebook for Deploying Distributed Renewable Energy Systems: As Case Study on the Cobrador Hybrid Solar PV Minigrid* (ADB 2019)

5. *Improving Lives of Rural Communities Through Developing Small Hybrid Renewable Energy Systems* (ADB 2017)

6. *Microsoft Excel-Based Tool Kit for Planning Hybrid Energy Systems: A User Guide* (ADB 2017)

3.2 Interconnected Microgrids

At the highest level, the philosophy behind interconnected microgrids is somewhat analogous to the practice of mitigating risk and lowering the cost of capital, by investing in a diversified portfolio of similar projects rather than a single project. Similar comparisons can be made to pooling in resource management. Microgrids can be interconnected to potentially further improve their efficiency, reliability, resilience, sustainability, and safety. However, since microgrids work in real time with multiple variables and processes, interconnection can lead to a sharp increase in system complexity. In line with the aforementioned advantages, two potential applications of interconnected minigrids could include:

1. Interconnected minigrids for minimizing the load shedding in a microgrid during islanded operation. Similarly, islanded neighbor microgrids can be interconnected if they are on a "self-healing"[16] smart grid network, and extra generation capacity by way of DERs is available in at least one of those microgrids. Interconnection means that the total load in the system of interconnected microgrids can be shared by all the DERs within these microgrids. However, for this to happen while maintaining stable operation, a carefully designed self-healing and supply restoration control algorithm, as well as requisite protection systems and communication infrastructure, are required at the network and microgrid levels (Shahnia et al. 2014).

2. When the level of variable renewable energy penetration increases in the power grid, larger voltage and frequency fluctuations appear in distribution systems. To mitigate this, microgrids with energy storage are a potential solution. However, existing designs are not very cost-effective for handling large power fluctuations unless high capacities of relatively costly energy storage are incorporated. Zhou et al. (2019) describe a flexible multi-microgrid interconnection scheme that can potentially optimize the pooled utilization of energy storage across multiple interconnected microgrids as a way to address this cost hurdle, albeit with slightly increased expense for AC/DC converters and DC lines construction, which is most economically viable when distances between the interconnected microgrids are short.

Milligrids are an extension of the pooling philosophy behind interconnected microgrids. However, in this case, a portion of the existing utility is utilized, with shared distribution power paths being harnessed to connect dispersed DERs, which do not fall within the clear geographical boundary of a traditional microgrid.[17]

3.3 Areas for Additional Technical Research

Microgrids currently have certain open areas for additional technical research (Planas et al. 2015). Some of the key aspects include:

(i) Applicable to both AC and DC microgrids:

(a) **Decentralized control.** Most of the existing microgrids around the world use centralized control. This type of control is optimal for small microgrids in which all the elements share the same goals. As these elements present different needs and the microgrid gets more complex, the alternative of decentralized control becomes more suitable. Thus, additional research is needed to develop the decentralized control approach.

---

[16] Network architecture that can withstand failure in its transmission paths by automatically correcting the fault.

[17] For example, Baltimore Gas and Electric (BGE) tested the Edmondson Village Area Milligrid in 2016, which is essentially a community microgrid in downtown Baltimore that can supply backup power to public buildings and local retail businesses and that can double up as emergency shelters when needed. It is a technically milligrid, rather than the community microgrid application that it serves, because it involves multiple points on BGE's grid that are not necessarily in the same boundary. A milligrid often does not have a single point of connection with the utility grid, which is characteristic of most microgrids.

(b) **Protections.** Microgrids are able to operate connected or disconnected from the main grid at any time. This dynamic scheme complicates the design of the protection scheme which must guarantee a safe operation in any case. Although some protection schemes have been proposed, they are customized solutions that do not provide a standardized approach for applicable to any microgrid.

(ii) DC microgrids also required specific research efforts in the following issues:

(a) **Bus selection.** The bus selection procedure is based on switching mechanisms that can lead to unwanted voltage oscillations. Achieving a smooth bus selection requires an appropriate control approach and implementation. Nowadays, there are few works that deal with this problem, thus more research efforts are needed.

(b) **Standards.** The standardization of AC microgrids has improved in the last few years. DC microgrids on the other hand, do not have yet a specific standard. Some organizations[18] have already taken the first steps into standardization of DC distribution lines.

(c) **Islanding detection techniques:** Islanding detection is a key requirement for electrical safety and equipment protection. Islanding detection algorithms in AC systems are based on systems frequency and phase parameters that are not present in DC lines. Thus, new methods for islanding detection in DC systems are required to guarantee the reliability of the system.

3.4 Transactive Energy

Transactive energy can be described as an electricity ecosystem comprised of multiple participants (e.g., decentralized generators, loads, and storage) interacting with each other, bound by a set of common economic and control mechanisms, but with potentially competing goals and objectives, to facilitate a dynamic balance of supply and demand across the entire electrical infrastructure using value as a key operational parameter. Transactive energy techniques may be localized to managing a specific geographical (e.g., microgrid), or functional (e.g., residential DR for the utility grid), part of the power system. In addition, studies and pilots have also proposed transactive energy for managing end-to-end (generation to consumption) activity at the larger electric power system level. Figure 41 presents a simplified pictorial depiction of transactive energy operations.

Figure 41: Transactive Energy Operations Overview

Source: Smart Electric Power Alliance (SEPA). 2019. *Transactive Energy: Real World Applications for the Modern Grid.* https://sepapower.org/resource/transactive-energy-real-world-applications-for-the-grid/.

---

[18]   Such as EPRI and Emerge Alliance.

With the increased proliferation of DERs, DSM, energy storage, and decentralized networks such as microgrids, in the evolving smart grid, there is significant potential for cost, efficiency, and resource utilization improvements through the enabling of market-based transactive exchanges between energy producers and consumers. In fact, as the penetration of the aforementioned grid edge components increases beyond a point, the lack of control and visibility to the centralized utility, if not addressed, can begin to pose serious planning, operational, and oversight challenges due to increased output fluctuations, voltage and reactive power variation, and reverse power flows in stage 3, and to an extent, stage 2, of Figure 42. While most distribution systems in the world are still in stage 1, the transactive energy systems approach offers great potential to address the challenges, and capitalize on the opportunities that stages 2 and 3 will bring.

Figure 42: Grid Evolution

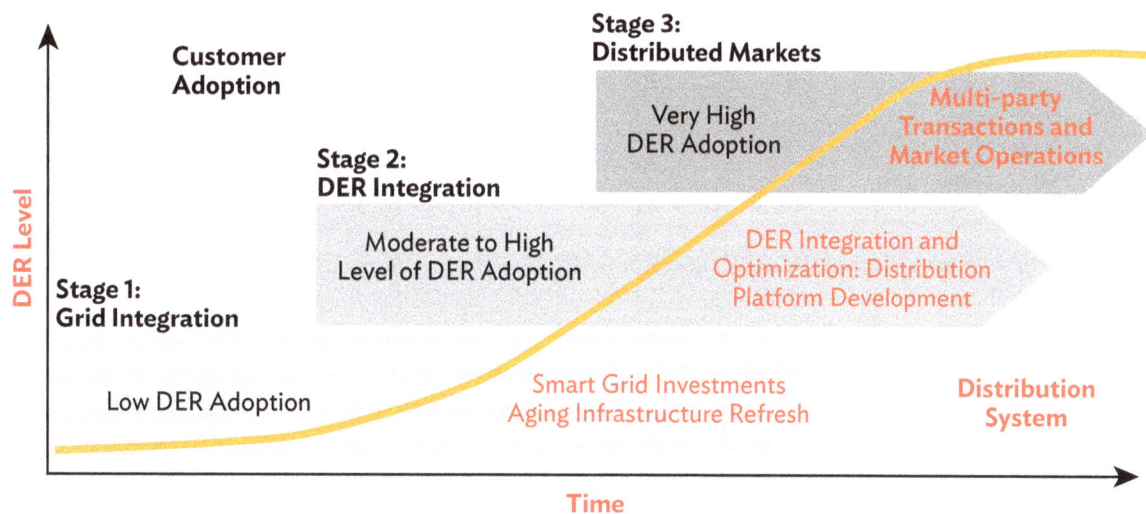

DER = distributed energy resource.

Note: A summary of transactive energy case studies, including one at a microgrid project, appears in Appendix 6.

Source: Smart Electric Power Alliance (SEPA). 2019. *Transactive Energy: Real World Applications for the Modern Grid.* https://sepapower.org/resource/transactive-energy-real-world-applications-for-the-grid/.

3.4.1 Peer-to-Peer Energy Trading

Microgrids have the technical capability to support multi-parameter energy trading within them, provided there is an efficient energy market model and robust secure standards to support it. Transactive energy can facilitate such a peer-to-peer (P2P) energy trading mechanism, within microgrids and between interconnected microgrids, among distributed generation, loads, and energy storage resources, that operate rationally and in self-interest. This can in turn raise the microgrids' efficiency and asset utilization rate. While pilots and studies exist, there appears to be limited documentation of any in commercial operation.

3.4.2 Blockchain Technologies

Blockchain is an "open, distributed ledger that can record transactions between two parties efficiently and in a verifiable and permanent way" (Iansiti and Lakhani 2017). Blockchain has value to the energy sector (Table 14). Perhaps the single most important blockchain tool for the energy sector is smart contracts, of which an overview is shown is Appendix 9.

Table 14: Applications of Blockchain to Cleantech

		Financing Infrastructure	Visibility and Alignment	Awareness and Access
Mobilizing new sources of financing	Decentralized infrastructure financing	main focus		
	Carbon-offsetting platform	main focus		
Emissions identification and certification	Ghg emissions certificate trading		main focus	
	Virtual carbon content accounting		main focus	
	Certificates of origin for green power		main focus	
	Agricultural and natural land screening		main focus	
Mobilizing consumers in regards to mitigation and adaptation	Rewards-market for GHG-reductions		main focus	main focus
	Food provenance for consumer visibility		main focus	main focus
	Efficient recycling systems to support a circular economy approach	secondary focus		main focus
	Seamless access to electrical vehicle charging			main focus
	Disaster risk insurance			main focus
Enabling the efficient use of current infrastructure systems	Traffic management platforms		main focus	
	Power sharing economy (p2p trading)		main focus	
	Global logistics capacity trading		main focus	

■ main focus   ■ secondary focus   limited focus

GHG = greenhouse gas, P2P = peer-to-peer.
Source: Organisation for Economic Co-operation and Development (OECD). 2019. *Blockchain Technologies as a Digital Enabler for Sustainable Infrastructure.* OECD Directorate for Financial and Enterprise Affairs.

In the context of transactive energy and P2P energy trading, blockchain technology solutions offer potential answers to many of the most vexing questions facing utilities, microgrids operators, grid edge resources, power system operators, and emerging competitors alike, including:

(i)   How are new markets going to be constructed that reflect the dynamic, decentralized structures of the new electricity system?
(ii)   How are "prosumers" of today and tomorrow to be incentivized and rewarded for either conserving energy or producing and trading energy?
(iii) How are transactions and information flows across a decentralized electricity network adequately secured?
(iv)   How do we move to more open-sourced application development environments to encourage more innovation in the electricity sector?

An overview of use cases in the power and utility operations sector including clean energy, is shown in Figure 43.

Additional illustration on the microgrid blockchain use case is in Appendix 10.

Figure 43: Blockchain Use Cases in Power and Utilities Sector

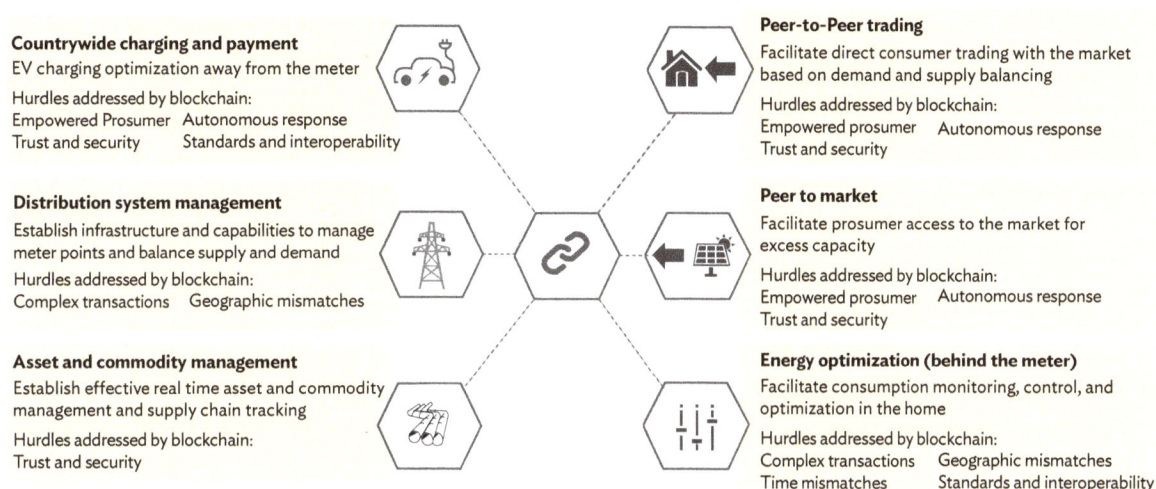

Countrywide charging and payment
EV charging optimization away from the meter

Hurdles addressed by blockchain:
Empowered Prosumer   Autonomous response
Trust and security   Standards and interoperability

Distribution system management
Establish infrastructure and capabilities to manage meter points and balance supply and demand
Hurdles addressed by blockchain:
Complex transactions   Geographic mismatches

Asset and commodity management
Establish effective real time asset and commodity management and supply chain tracking
Hurdles addressed by blockchain:
Trust and security

Peer-to-Peer trading
Facilitate direct consumer trading with the market based on demand and supply balancing

Hurdles addressed by blockchain:
Empowered prosumer   Autonomous response
Trust and security

Peer to market
Facilitate prosumer access to the market for excess capacity

Hurdles addressed by blockchain:
Empowered prosumer   Autonomous response
Trust and security

Energy optimization (behind the meter)
Facilitate consumption monitoring, control, and optimization in the home

Hurdles addressed by blockchain:
Complex transactions   Geographic mismatches
Time mismatches   Standards and interoperability

EV = electric vehicle.

Source: Nandapawar, H. 2018. *Blockchain—Smart Disruption for Clean Energy Deployment*. Manila: ADB; Asia Clean Energy Forum 2018.

Given that some readers may be additionally interested in blockchain's potential energy infrastructure investment facilitation aspects that go beyond the microgrids operation and energy trading emphasis of this section, three possible use cases for the former could be:

(i) The concept of "tokenizing" renewable energy assets as a way to democratize financing has broad, intuitive appeal. Tokenization is often mentioned toward the rear of an energy-blockchain startup's white paper, or in the later phases of a product road map. It does not offer the same appeal as P2P trading, but is an important concept in the blockchain world.

(ii) Blockchain, with its distributed ledger, smart contracts and tradable tokens on exchanges that have no technical limits on their geographic scope, does appear to offer a platform that improves on the crowdfunding trend.

(iii) Monitoring of renewable energy certificate and natural gas markets, may be the first of these use cases to commercialize.

Despite the promising potential, blockchain is a means to an end and not the end it itself. It is also not a silver bullet solution. For instance, questions for regulators and policy makers to consider include to what extent blockchain represents a disruption or smooth transition for incumbent utilities; and whether the current enterprise software providers are up to the task of making a paradigm shift, or if new entrants will lead this evolution. There are also limitations to the scenarios in which it is practical to use blockchain:

1. For many potential applications, the value of blockchain is additive, but not revolutionary.
   - Blockchain can empower individual consumers to produce energy and trade directly with other consumers in their network, enabling better access to local energy.
   - Blockchain-based systems do not eradicate the requirement for a market platform.

2. As it scales, blockchain cannot escape regulatory and operational standards already in place.
   - Currently, ISOs verify that the electricity system can carry out the flow and trade of electrons, and they effectively match buyers and sellers to meet load and demand. All transactions must be verified with the ISO, which takes the physical constraints of the system into account when settling transactions and dispatching resources in real time.

3. Even if all market and operational constraints could be represented in a blockchain platform, ISOs constantly monitor the system—rethinking and changing the rules, and occasionally intervening in the market.

    –   The blockchain platform could just be used as tool used by the ISO to process trades.

    –   If the idea is to replace the ISO, there might be additional implications of a totally free and transparent market for electricity.

4. Some might argue in favor of using permissioned, or closed, blockchains as opposed to public, or open, blockchains.

    –   Permissioned blockchains limit who can contribute to the ledger and manage the data. ISOs need to be in charge of the electricity system; therefore, a permissioned blockchain would allow regulators to monitor inputs.

    –   In contrast, the trustless nature of a public blockchain is not practical for energy applications.

5. Transmission constraints are another hurdle, as a distribution system is not designed for two-way flows. Peer-to-peer trading is niche at the moment, but if transactions ramp up, utilities will need to interfere to maintain the system's status quo.

6. This issue doesn't arise when trading bitcoin or Ethereum, as cryptocurrencies need not rely on transmission lines and physical constraints.
    –   Electricity differs from finance in that it is more than a market: It is a system complete with physical infrastructure and the limitations that come with it.

    –   Though transactive energy using blockchain is an attractive idea, many companies seem to feel it is many years away from becoming a commercial reality.

Appendix 11 shows a general decision flowchart that can guide a bottom-up decision-making process on the use of blockchain.

3.5 Internet of Things, Data Analytics, and Artificial Intelligence

The Internet of Things (IoT) is a large global dynamic network infrastructure of internet-enabled, always on, web services-enabled entities. Smart grid is an important application of IoT, which along with data analytics, and artificial intelligence are ongoing research areas that have the potential to translate into significant incremental benefits for microgrid capabilities and thereby a microgrid's techno-commercial viability. Essentially, microgrids are comprised of equipment that require a huge amount of sensors, connectivity (both constituents of IoT), and self-learning (attained via data analytics and artificial intelligence), to perform at its best. Smart grid integrable IoT architectures typically have three or four layers as shown in Table 15.

Table 15: Layers Proposed for Internet of Things Architecture in a Smart Grid

	Model 1	Model 2	Model 3	Model 4	Typical Devices
Layer 4		Application	Social	Master station system	Artificial intelligence systems to provide information to decision and billing systems
Layer 3	Application	Cloud management	Application	Remote Communication	
Layer 2	Network	Network	Network	Field network	Devices for receiving data at central system
Layer 1	Perception	Perception	Perception	Terminal	Smart meters, network devices, communication protocols

Source: Ghasempour, A. 2019. Internet of Things in Smart Grid: Architecture, Applications, Services, Key Technologies, and Challenges. *Inventions*. 4(22). doi:doi:10.3390/inventions4010022.

The sort of data that could be gathered, analyzed, and acted upon, includes energy usage patterns, grid tariff rates, solar PV output, and weather predictions. Examples of applications that this data and capabilities could be used in include:

1. Improved fault detection, reliability, and resilience, such as
   - optimizing line voltage to minimize energy losses and line damage;
   - locating the source of sags, surges, and outages;
   - improving load balancing, restoring services faster, and making safer override decisions;
   - identifying the source of technical and nontechnical losses in the system, reducing the costs of service;
   - lowering outage investigation times by isolating fault locations; and,
   - improving asset management, and preventive and predictive maintenance with AI.

2. Improved energy management
   - Smart battery charging and discharging systems that use a self-learning algorithm with AI to optimize performance;
   - Improved DSM and DR programs that incorporate AI to deduce predicted market or customer behaviors;
   - Monitor DER generation along with emissions, storage, consumption, etc. and predict the electricity requirement; and
   - Integrate with EV management systems.

3. AI in microgrid controllers
   - improved control, drawing on historical and real-time data from microgrid sensors, meters, and other equipment, as well as from weather stations and weather data feeds.

APPENDIX 1
Main Technologies of Renewable Distributed Generators

Main Technologies of Renewable Distributed Generators

Energy-based Technology Type	Primary Energy	Output Type	Module Power (Kw)	Electrical Efficiency (%)	Overall Efficiency (%)	Advantages	Disadvantages
Wind	Wind	AC	0.2-3000	_a	~50-80	✓ Day and night power generation	✗ Still expensive
						✓ One of the most developed renewable energy technology	✗ Storage mechanisms required
Photovoltaic systems	Sun	DC	0.02-1000	_a	~40-45	✓ Emission free	✗ Storage mechanisms required
						✓ Useful in a variety of applications	✗ High up-front cost
Biomass gasification	Biomass	AC	100-20,000	15-25	~60-75	✓ Minimal environmental impact	
						✓ Available throughout the world	✗ Still expensive
						✓ Alcohols and other fuels produced by biomass are efficient, viable, nd relatively clean burning	✗ A net loss of energy in small scale
Small hydro power	Water	AC	5-100,000	_a	~90-98	✓ Economic and environmentally friendly	✗ Suitable site characteristics required
						✓ Relatively low up-front investment costs and maintenance	✗ Difficult energy expansion
						✓ Useful for providing peak power and spinning reserves	✗ Environmental impact
Geothermal	Hot water	AC	5000-100,000	Oct-32	~35-50	✓ Extremely environmentally friendly	✗ Non-availability of geothermal spots in the land of interest
						✓ Low running costs	
Ocean energy	Ocean wave	AC	10-1000	_a	_a	✓ High power density	✗ Lack of commercial projects
						✓ More predictable than solar or wind	✗ Unknown operations and maintenance costs
Solar thermal	Sun and water	AC	1000-80,000	30-40	~50-75	✓ Simple, low maintenance	✗ Unknown operations and maintenance costs
						✓ Operating costs nearly zero	✗ Low energy density
						✓ Mature technology	✗ Limited scalability

_a = No data available, AC = alternating current, DC = direct current.

Source: Planas, E. et al. 2015. *AC and DC Technology in Microgrids: A Review. Renewable and Sustainable Energy Reviews.* 43: pp. 726–749. https://doi.org/10.1016/j.rser.2014.11.067.

Main Technologies of Nonrenewable Distributed Generators

Main Technologies of Nonrenewable Distributed Generators							
Energy-based Technology Type	Primary Energy	Output Type	Module Power (Kw)	Electrical Efficiency (%)	Overall Efficiency (%)	Advantages	Disadvantages
Reciprocating engines	Diesel or gas	AC	3-6000	30-43	~80-85	✓ Low cost	✗ Environmentally unfriendly emissions
						✓ High efficiency	
						✓ Ability to use various inputs	
						✓ Useful in a variety of applications	✗ High up-front cost
Gas turbine	Diesel or gas	AC	0.5-30,000	21-40	~80-90	✓ High efficiencies when using CHP	✗ Too big for small consumers
						✓ Environmentally friendly	
						✓ Cost effective	
Micro-turbine	Bio-gas, propane, or natural gas	AC	30-1000	14-30	~80-85	✓ Small size and light weight	✗ Expensive technology
						✓ Easy start-up and shut-down	✗ Cost-effectiveness sensitive to the price of fuel
						✓ Low maintenance costs	✗ Environmentally unfriendly emissions
Fuel cell	Ethanol, H2, N2, natural gas, PEM, phosphoric acid, or propane	DC	1-20,000	05-55	~80-90	✓ One of the most environmentally friendly generators	✗ Extracting hydrogen is expensive
						✓ Extremely quiet	✗ Expensive infrastructure for hydrogen
						✓ Useful for combined heat and electricity applications	

AC = alternating current, DC = direct current, H2 = hydrogen, N2 = Nitrogen, PEM =polymer electrolyte membrane.

Source: Planas, E. et al. 2015. *AC and DC Technology in Microgrids: A Review. Renewable and Sustainable Energy Reviews.* 43: pp. 726–749. https://doi.org/10.1016/j.rser.2014.11.067.

APPENDIX 3
Main Technologies of Storage Systems Used in Microgrids

Technology	Efficiency (%)	Capacity (MW)	Energy density (Wh/kg)	Capital (€/kW)	Lifetime (years)	Maturity	Environmental Impact	Examples
TES[a]	30–60	0–300	80–250	140–220	5–40	Developed	Small	Solar two Central Receiver Power Plant, California (US)
PHS[b]	75–85	100–5,000	0.5–1.5	400–1500	40–60	Mature	Negative	Rocky River PHS Plant, Hartford (US)
CAES[c]	50–85	3–400	30–60	250–1500	20–60	Developed	Negative	Huntorf (Germany) and McIntosh, Alabama (US)
Flywheel	93–95	0–25	10–30	250	~15	Demonstration	Almost	Commercially supplied by AFS-Trinity (US), Beacon Power (US), Piller (US), etc.
Pbacid battery[d]	70–90	0–40	30–50	200	5–15	Mature	Negative	BEWAG Plant, Berlin (Germany)
NiCd battery[e]	60–65	0–40	50–75	350–1,100	10–20	Commercial	Negative	Golden Valley, Alaska (US)
NaS nbattery[f]	80–90	0.05–8	150–240	700–2,100	10–15	Commercial	Negative	Tokyo Electric Power Company (Japan)
Li-ion battery[g]	85–90	0–1	75–200	3,000	5–15	Demonstration	Negative	Kyushu Electric Power and Mitsubishi Heavy Industries (Japan)
Fuel cells	20–50	0–50	800–10,000	350–1,100	5–15	Developing	Small	Topsoe Fuel Cell, Lyngby (Denmark)
Flow battery	75–85	0.3–15	10–50	400–1,100	5–15	Developing	Negative	Innogys Little Barford Power Station (UK)
Capacitors	60–65	0–0.05	0.05–5	250	~5	Developed	Small	Commercially supplied by SAFT (France), NESS (Republic of Korea), ESMA (Russian Federation) etc.
Supercapacitators	90–95	0–0.3	2.5–15	200	> 20	Developed	Small	PowerCache (Maxwell, US), ELIT (Russian Federation), PowerSystem Co. (Japan), Chubu Electric Power (Japan), etc.
SMES[h]	95–98	0.1–10	0.5–5	200	> 20	Demonstration	Positive	Wisconsin Public Service Corporation (US)

UK = United Kingdom, US = United States.

[a] TES: thermal energy storage.

[b] PHS: pumped hydro storage.
[c] CAES: compressed air energy storage.
[d] Pb-acid battery: lead-acid battery.
[e] Ni-Cd battery: nickel-cadmium battery.
[f] Na-S battery: sodium-sulfur battery.
[g] Li-ion battery: lithium-ion battery.
[h] SMES: Superconducting magnetic energy storage.

Source: Planas, E. et al. 2015. *AC and DC Technology in Microgrids: A Review. Renewable and Sustainable Energy Reviews.* 43: pp. 726–749. https://doi.org/10.1016/j.rser.2014.11.067.

APPENDIX 4
Standards for Alternating Current and Direct Current Microgrids

Type	Standard	Description	Scopes
AC and DC	IEEE 1547	Criteria and requirements for interconnection of DERs with the main grid	1547.1 Conformance test
			1547.2 Application guide
			1547.3 Monitoring and control
			1547.4 Design, operation, and integration of DERs
			1547.5 Interconnection guidelines for electric power sources greater than 10 MVA
			1547.6 Interconnection with distribution secondary networks
			1547.7 Distribution impact studies for interconnection of DERs
			1547.8 Recommended practice for establishing methods and procedures
AC	EN 50160	Voltage characteristics of electricity supplied by public distribution networks	Definitions and indicative values for a number of power quality phenomena in LV and MV networks
			Limits for power frequency, voltage variations, harmonics voltage, voltage unbalance, flicker, and mains signalling
	IEC 61000	General conditions or rules necessary for achieving electromagnetic compatibility	Safety function and integrity requirements
			Compatibility levels
			Emission and immunity limits
			Measurement and testing techniques
			Installation guidelines, mitigation methods and devices
	IEEE C37.95	Protective relaying of utility-consumer interconnections	Establishment of consumer service requirements and supply methods
			Protection system design considerations
DC	ETSI EN 300 132-3-1	Environmental engineering (EE), Power supply interface at the input to information and communication technology (ICT) equipment; Part 3; Subpart 1: Direct currenty source up to 400 V	Definition of DC interface up to DC 400 V
			DC bus voltage limits consideration
			Guidelines for testing powered equipment behavior for abnormal operating conditions and stress
	EPRI and Emergence	Standard for 400 Vdc in buildings (under construction)	Interiors and occupied spaces where lighting and control loads dominate the need for DC electricity
			Data centres and telecom central offices with their DC-powered information and communication technology equipment
			Outdoor electrical uses, including electric vehicle charging and outdoor light-emitting diode (LED) lighting
			Building services, utilities, and HVAC with variable-speed drive and electronic DC motorized equipment

continued on next page

Table *continued*

Type	Standard	Description	Scopes
	IEC SG4	LVDC distribution system up to 1500 V (under construction)	Align and coordinate activities in many areas where LVDC is used such as green data centers, commercial buildings, electricity storage for all mobile products (with batteries), electric vehicles, and so forth, including all mobile products with batteries, lighting, multimedia, ICT, etc. with electronic supply units
			Measuring methods
			Architecture: 100% DC or hybrid
			Grounding
			Operation and life cycle of the equipment
			Protective measurements for hazard for LVDC distribution systems
			The impact of DC (corrosion, insulation, etc.)

AC = alternating current; DC = direct current; DER = distributed energy resources; HVAC = heating, ventilation, and air conditioning; LV = low voltage; MV = medium voltage; MVA = mega volt-ampere.

Notes:
(i)   IEEE 1547 is a set of technical specifications that defines the performance and functionalities of DER connected to the distribution grid—the part of the electric grid that delivers power to homes and buildings. This technology-neutral standard provides uniform requirements for the safe interconnection of DER to the grid and details the associated testing needed for interconnection.
    (a)   IEEE 1547 is being expanded to accommodate microgrids.
    (b)   IEEE 1547 anti-islanding requirements are viewed as a barrier for renewable based microgrids.
    (c)   IEEE 1547.8 working group focuses on microgrids, high penetration DG and advanced inverters.
(ii) EN 50160, describes the voltage characteristics of the electricity supplied by public distribution networks. In particular, this is an important standard for voltage characteristics as it provides information on power quality, frequency and voltage variations such as voltage sag and swell, unbalanced voltage and current flows and harmonics in microgrids.
(iii) IEC 61000 is about general conditions or rules necessary for achieving safety function and integrity requirements related to electromagnetic compatibility.
(iv) IEEE C37.95 describes the protective relaying of utility-consumer interconnections.
(v)   IEEE 37.188 is the IEEE standard for synchro-phasors in power systems.
(vi) OpenADR is a standard for Automated Demand-Response

Source: Planas, E. et al. 2015. *AC and DC Technology in Microgrids: A Review. Renewable and Sustainable Energy Reviews.* 43: pp. 726–749. https://doi.org/10.1016/j.rser.2014.11.067.

APPENDIX 5
Alternating Current and Direct Current Microgrid Control Strategies

Operating Mode	AC Microgrids	DC Microgrids
Grid-connected mode		
	■ Monitoring sytem diagnosis by collecting information from the LVAC network, DG units and loads (AC and DC).	■ The main function of the MGCC is to independently control the power flow and load-end voltage profile of the DG units in response to any disturbance and load changes.
MGCC	■ Performance state estimation and security assessments, evaluate economic generation scheduling, active and reactive power control of the DGs units and demand side management functions using the available information.	■ Participating in economic generation scheduling, load tracking or management and demand side management (DSM) by controlling the storage devices.
	■ Ensuring synchronized operation with the main grid, maintaining the power exchange at prior contract points.	
DGCs	■ Ensuring that each DG unit rapidly picks up its generation to supply its share of the load in stand-alone mode and comes back to the grid-connected mode automatically with the help of the MGCC.	■ Ensuring that each DG unit quickly picks up its generation to supply its share of the load in stand-alone mode and comes back to the grid-connected mode automatically with the help of MGCC.
Islanding mode		
	■ Performing active and reactive power control of the DGs to maintain stable voltage and frequency at the load ends.	■ Independently control the power flow and load-end voltage profile of the DG units in response to any disturbance and load changes.
MGCC	■ Managing load interruption/shedding strategies using demand side management (DSM) with ESS support for maintaining power balance and voltage.	■ Ensuring the DG units rapidly picks up its generation to supply its local load in islanding mode and automatically reconnect to grid with the help of the MGCC.
	■ Initializing local black start to ensure reliability and continuity of the service.	
	■ Switching the microgrid to grid-connected mode after the main grid supply is restored without hampering the stability of either grid.	
DGCs	■ Commanding each DG unit to rapidly pick up its generation to supply its corresponding local loads in the stand-alone mode and automatically resynchronize to grid with the help of the MGCC.	■ Ensuring that each DG unit rapidly picks up its generation to supply its share of the loads in stand-alone mode and comes back to the grid-connected mode automatically with the help of the MGCC.

AC = alternating current, DC = direct current, DGC = distribute generation controller, LVAC = low voltage AC, MGCC = microgrid central controller.

Source: Justo, J. J. and F. Mwasilu. 2013. *AC-Microgrids versus DC-Microgrids with Distributed Energy Resources: A Review. Renewable and Sustainable Energy Reviews.* https://www.researchgate.net/publication/270831774.

APPENDIX 6
Transactive Energy Case Studies Summary

PROJECT NAME	Distribution System Platform Pilot	Microgrid Project	Olympic Peninsula Demonstration Project	Retailed Automated Transactive Energy System Pilot
COMPANY	National Grid & Opus One	Introspective Systems	Pacific Northwest National Laboratory	TeMix Inc., Universal Devices Inc. & Southern California Edison
LOCATION	Buffalo, New York	Isle au Haut, Maine	Olympic Peninsula, Washington State	Thousand Oaks, California
PARTICIPANT	1	140	112	100
TECHNOLOGIES	Combined heat and power, responsive demand, and existing back-up generators (energy storage and renewable generation are under evaluation).	Solar, blockchain, battery, diesel generator (backup), microgrid controller, heat pumps with thermal storage, and inverters	Residential demand response from electric water systems, space heaters, water pumps, and diesel generator (backup).	AC, heat pumps, pool pumps, batteries, UDI home automation controller (UDI EMS ISY), TeMix Platform, software (TeMix Agent), smart meters
DRIVERS	Legislation (New York REV)	Low costs	Avoiding or delaying a transmission upgrade (due to capacity contraints)	High solar penetration (leading to negative prices or curtailment), greenhouse gas reduction, the state's desire to electrify buildings and EVs
WHAT WORKED	Demonstrated they can calculate the distribution value of energy with the DSP platform and successful program enrollment.	Doing simulations with multivariate co-optimization to figure out how to offer lowest cost; use of fractal smart ledger blockchain with a permissioned network for distributing the ledger to transfer the distributed generation value; and pricing network with one-way pricing signals.	Succesful management of congestion on a distribution circuit; demonstrated that TE can enable wholesale price purchases by utility; generators, loads, and appliances could automatically bid into a real-time energy market, achieving cost savings across customer segments.	Automated transactions based on price signals. Minimization of customer participation.
CHALLENGES	Initial pilot location. Limited data availability and granularity. Lack of standardized communication protocols.	Getting people to see that TE can play a role in our grid distribution system. Getting accurate battery vendor information.	Reliable communication. Modifying appliances for any unique response capability (or any single pilot). Lack of interoperability (smart device integration took longer than expected). Few customers changed their given options after smart equipment was integrated into their homes.	Recruiting customers before system is ready. Establishing approval of tariffs. Wireless communication issues. Meters not communicating. Some device vendors not having incentive to work with RATES.
LESSONS LEARNED	Communication protocols should be standardized.	Super capacitors work well for grid applications; when trying to produce a grid architecture that is self-stabilizing, care must be taken that unintended consequences do not arise as a result of the chosen contral algorithms.	A portfolio of price-flexible energy technologies is superior to any single offering; residents spend little time either understanding their energy bill or the nuanced transactive controls; appliance manufacturers need to maintain control of their devices and protect consumer experiences.	Deploy transactive platform, transactive tariff, and device agents before recruiting device vendors and customers; need more year-round flexible devices, such as batteries, electric heat pumps, EVs, and electric water heaters; RATES works and can be a component of California's retail electricity market with very high renewables penetration, storage, and customer response.

AC = alternating current, EV = electric vehicle, TE = transactive energy.

Source: Smart Electric Power Alliance (SEPA). 2019. *Transactive Energy: Real World Applications for the Modern Grid.* https://sepapower.org/resource/transactive-energy-real-world-applications-for-the-grid/.

APPENDIX 7
Blockchain Smart Contracts

The advantage of blockchain-based contracts is that they reduce the amount of human involvement required to create, execute, and enforce a contract, thereby lowering its cost while raising the assurance of execution and enforcement processes. By automating a transaction in a fully verifiable framework (the blockchain) the transactions can have legal validity even at high frequency—a key enabler for network balancing.

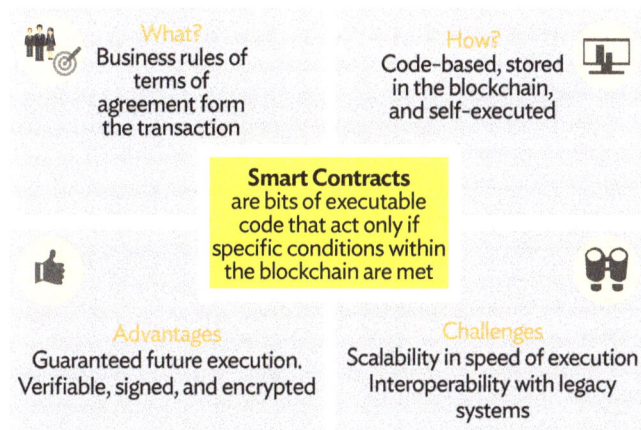

What?
Business rules of terms of agreement form the transaction

How?
Code-based, stored in the blockchain, and self-executed

Smart Contracts are bits of executable code that act only if specific conditions within the blockchain are met

Advantages
Guaranteed future execution. Verifiable, signed, and encrypted

Challenges
Scalability in speed of execution Interoperability with legacy systems

Traditional contracts	Smart contracts
1-3 Days	Minutes
Manual remittance	Automatic remittance
Escrow necessary	Escrow may not be necessary
Expensive	Fraction of the cost
Physical presence (wet signature)	Virtual presence (digital signature)
Lawyer necessary	Lawyer may not be necessary

Source: Nandapawar, H. 2018. *Blockchain—Smart Disruption for Clean Energy Deployment*. Manila: ADB; Asia Clean Energy Forum 2018.

Blockchain Microgrid Use Case

Blockchain can empower microgrids with limitless potential to have seamless integration with grid. Thereby enabling peer-to-peer trading—a key to unlocking finance.

▶ USE CASE: Microgrid - Reference: LO3ENERGY

● Consumer
● Solar renewable producer

— Consumption
- - Production

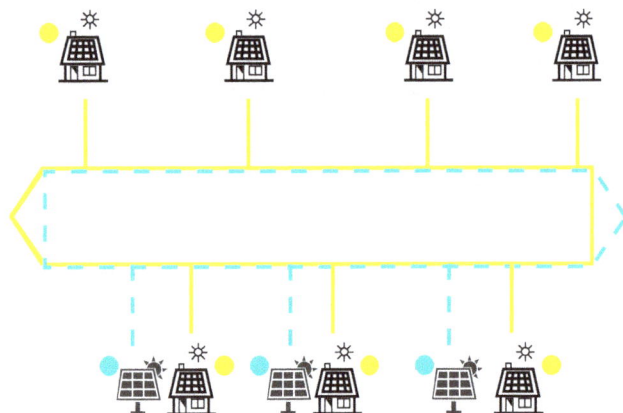

Role of blockchain?

▶ Blockchain facilities secure transactions of power between individuals on a distributed network who do not have an existing relationship
▶ Grid is based on an open source, cryptographically secure decentralized application platform
▶ All micro transactions are logged

How is blockchain used?

▶ Prosumers generate power beyond their needs and feed it into the grid using blockchain
▶ Real-time metering of local energy generation and usage as well as other related data
▶ Smart contracts automate agreed trading relationships, e.g., order of preference in community

What is the benefit?

▶ Enables reporting and self management on a real-time basis
▶ Consumers able to control who uses space generation
▶ Commercial transactions are auditable, improving trust

Source: Nandapawar, H. 2018. *Blockchain—Smart Disruption for Clean Energy Deployment*. Manila: ADB; Asia Clean Energy Forum 2018.

Bottom-Up Decision-Making Process on Using Blockchain

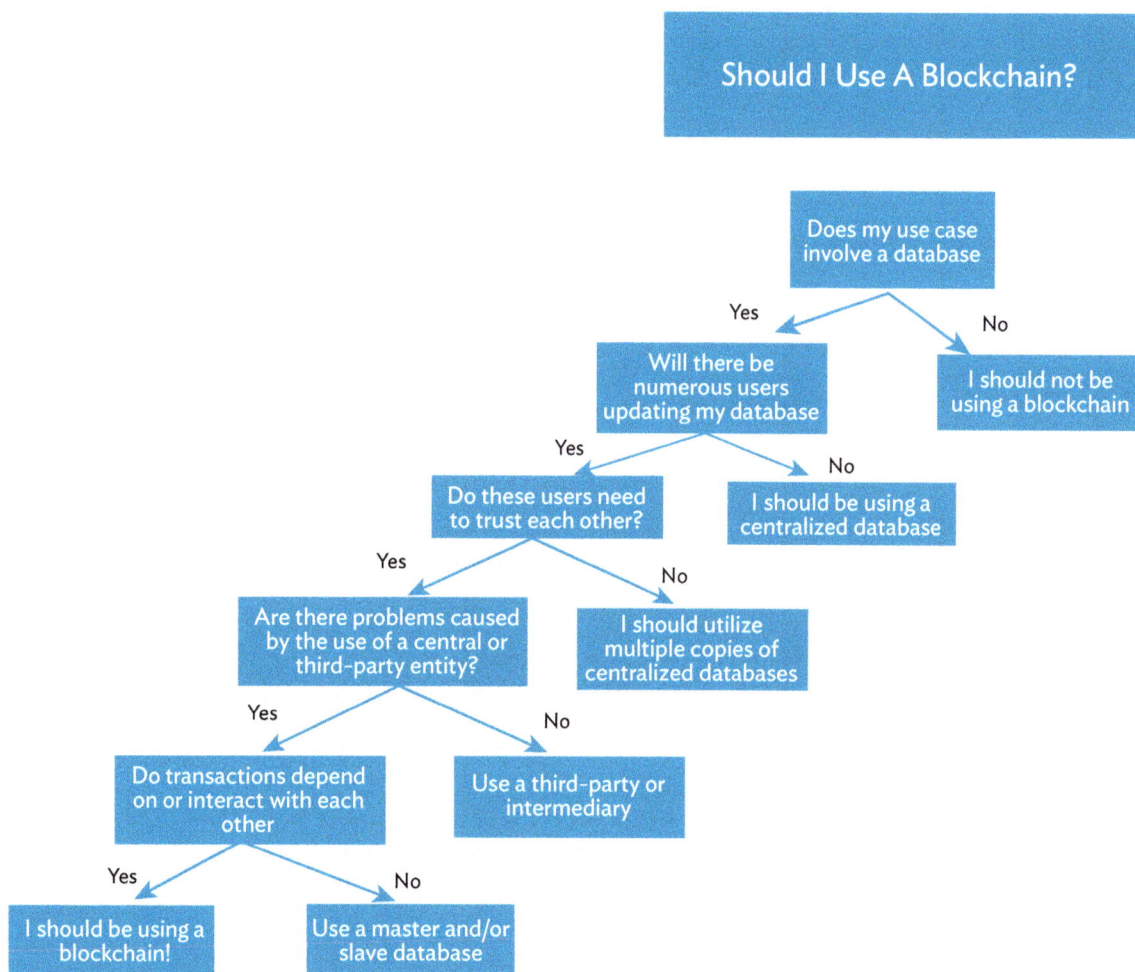

Should I Use A Blockchain?

Does my use case involve a database

Yes

No — **I should not be using a blockchain**

Will there be numerous users updating my database

Yes

No — **I should be using a centralized database**

Do these users need to trust each other?

Yes

No — **I should utilize multiple copies of centralized databases**

Are there problems caused by the use of a central or third-party entity?

Yes

No — **Use a third-party or intermediary**

Do transactions depend on or interact with each other

Yes — **I should be using a blockchain!**

No — **Use a master and/or slave database**

Source: Ett, Rachel. 2018. *Reality Check: Blockchain Needs Proof of Concept Before Revolutionizing the Grid.* https://www.greentechmedia.com/articles/read/reality-check-blockchain-needs-proof-of-concept-before-revolutionizing-the.

APPENDIX 10
Business Models – Detailed Description

Customer-Owned Model (Up-Front Capital Investment Model)

Figure A10.1: Capital Expenditure Investment Model

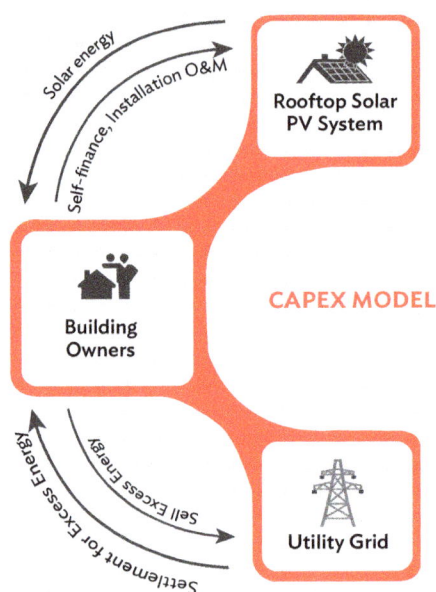

CAPEX = capital expenditure, PV = photovoltaic.

Source: EU-India Technical Cooperation Energy. http://www.pvrooftop.in/programme_info/05_business.htm.

In the Up-front Capital Investment model, the entire cost of installation of a microgrid asset, along with the responsibility of operation and maintenance (O&M) of the asset lie with the end energy consumer. The consumer typically invests its own resources (including borrowing from a bank or lender) and carries out the installation through an engineering, procurement, and construction (EPC) service provider. When the installation is complete, the consumer starts consuming the energy generated from microgrid asset. If there is a provision to export electricity to the grid, the consumer exports the excess electricity units into the grid for economic considerations. By replacing (often expensive) electricity units bought from the grid or diesel generators with lower-cost (typically renewable energy) generation, the consumer generates financial benefits on its investment through cost savings, once the initial capital investment is recovered from these savings (payback period).

In this model, the consumer may choose to invest its own capital resources or invest through a mix of external debt and equity. The consumer may also choose to carry out O&M of the asset through an in-house team or through a third-party O&M service provider. However, in this model, as a result of taking on the responsibility of making the necessary up-front investment and O&M, the consumer is exposed to any or all of the following risks:

(i)   Execution risk – risk of delays that may arise during engineering, procurement ,or construction (EPC) phase
(ii)   Performance risk – risk of less than expected outcome in the operational performance of microgrid asset over its useful life
(iii)   Technology risk – risk of a better and/or cheaper technology becoming available in the market after the investment is made

Renewable Energy Service Company-Owned Model

Figure A10.2: Renewable Energy Service Company-Owned Model

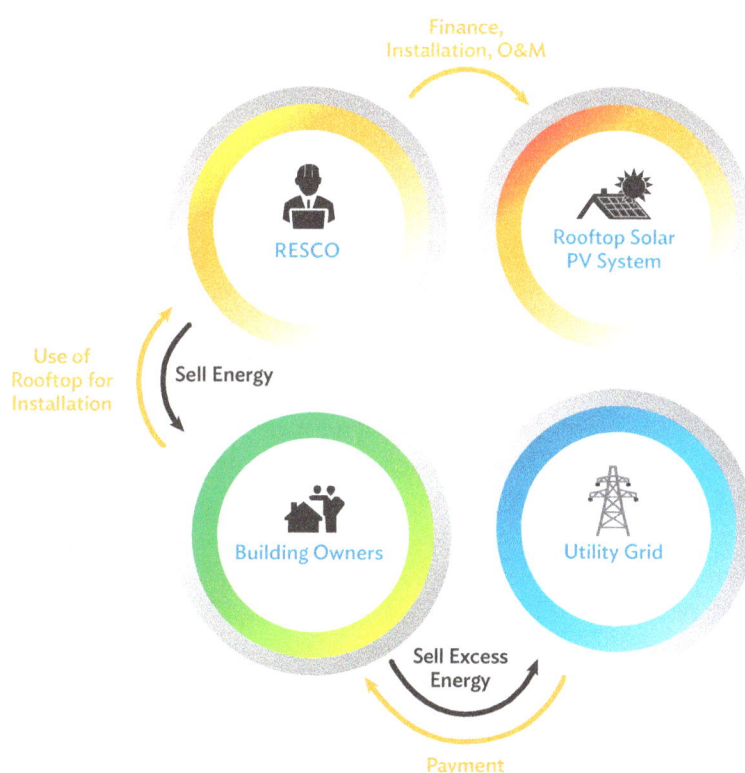

O&M = operation and maintenance, PV = photovoltaic, RESCO = renewable energy service company.
Source: EU-India Technical Cooperation Energy. http://www.pvrooftop.in/programme_info/05_business.htm.

In the RESCO model, the entire cost or at least a part of the cost of installation of microgrid asset along with the responsibility of O&M lie with a third party or a RESCO. Variations within this model exist, such as

(i)   Build-Own-Operate (BOO)
(ii)   Build-Own-Operate-Transfer (BOOT)
(iii)   Lease-to-own
(iv)   Power Purchase Agreement (PPA) model
(v)   Microgrid as a Service (MaaS) model

In this model, the responsibility of making necessary capital investment to build a microgrid asset and performing O&M lies with the RESCO. The RESCO and the consumer initially agree on the terms of engagement that typically includes tenor, price, price escalation, etc. and enter into a legally binding contract.

In case of the BOO variation of the RESCO model, the contract between the RESCO and the consumer is typically structured as fixed or variable periodic payments (monthly or annual) for energy services provided by the RESCO. The microgrid asset would be owned, maintained, and operated by the RESCO without ever transferring its ownership to the consumer. Any replacement or overhaul of the microgrid asset would also be the responsibility of the RESCO.

In case of the BOOT variation of the RESCO model, the contract between the RESCO and the consumer is typically structured as fixed or variable periodic payments for energy services provided by the RESCO, but for a pre-agreed fixed number of years. The microgrid asset would be owned, maintained, and operated by the RESCO until the validity of the contract. At the end of this contract's tenor, ownership of microgrid asset is transferred to the consumer, often on payment of a pre-agreed residual value of the asset to the RESCO. Any replacement or overhaul of microgrid asset would also be the responsibility of the RESCO during the contract's tenor, and any such overhaul would be the responsibility of the consumer after the end of the contract and ownership is transferred.

In case of the lease-to-own variation of the RESCO model, the contract between the RESCO and the consumer is typically structured as an 'operating lease' agreement or an 'energy savings performance' contract, wherein periodic payments would typically include the cost of energy services provided by the RESCO, as well as part-payments for the capital costs of microgrid asset, which are incurred up-front by the RESCO. At the end of the lease agreement, the capital cost of the microgrid asset would have been fully recovered by the RESCO, along with necessary margins to cover its O&M and financing costs, and the asset ownership would be transferred to the consumer. The lease-to-own model is often the contracting modality of BOOT model.

The PPA contracting structure is often employed in the BOO model, with the periodic payments to the RESCO being structured as a tariff per kilowatt hour (kWh) of electricity supplied by the RESCO to the consumer. Asset ownership remains with the RESCO forever, although in some cases, PPAs could be employed in the BOOT models too.

The MaaS model is similar to the BOO and BOOT models, wherein PPA or lease-to-own contracts can be used. However, MaaS models often use BOO with PPA contracts.

When the installation is complete, the consumer offsets (often expensive) electricity units from the grid and/or diesel generators with cheaper units generated by the microgrid asset, in line with the term of the lease or PPA or a similar contract. In the RESCO model, the consumer receives financial benefits in terms of cost savings from microgrid asset immediately since it has not made any up-front capital investments.

In this model, as a result of transferring the responsibility of investment and O&M to the RESCO, the consumer is protected from all of the following risks, since these risks are transferred to the RESCO:

(i)   Execution risk – risk of delays that may arise during EPC phase of microgrid installation
(ii)   Performance risk – risk of less than expected outcome in the operational performance of microgrid asset over its useful life
(iii) Technology risk – risk of a better and/or cheaper technology becoming available in the market after the investment is made

Nevertheless, it is important for the consumer to build sufficient risk mitigation and compensation measures into the contract with the RESCO to meet their electricity consumption and cost saving goals.

Utility-Owned Model

A utility-owned model is similar to the up-front capital investment model, except that the up-front capital investment and ownership of microgrid asset would be with the local utility, who would likely carry out the installation through an EPC service provider. Although some utilities have in-house EPC capabilities and they could complete the installation themselves too. When the installation is complete, the energy generated from microgrid asset would be supplied to local consumers of the utility. The utility may choose to pass on some of the cost savings due to the microgrid installation to its consumers, so that their electricity consumption costs may be lowered as well.

Often, utilities invest in grid-connected microgrid assets not just as a way to lower their electricity generation costs but also as a way to stabilize electricity supply at tail-ends of their grid and increase the efficiency of their system, since urban centers are often located far away from power generation assets and sources and due to long distance transmission and distribution losses, it may be more efficient and economical to set up microgrids that generate and distribute electricity locally, thereby eliminating transmission and distribution (T&D) losses.

Cooperative-Owned Model

A cooperative-owned model is similar to the up-front capital investment model, except that the up-front capital investment and ownership of microgrid asset would be the responsibility of a local cooperative, which would likely carry out the installation through an EPC service provider. The local cooperative is often a cooperative of local electricity consumers—typically C&I consumers—who come together to organize themselves into a cooperative to aggregate their electricity demand, thereby achieving larger scale microgrids that allow cost and operational efficiencies. When the installation is complete, the energy generated from microgrid asset would be supplied to local consumers, who are likely to be members of the cooperative that owns and operates the microgrid asset.

In some cases, a cooperative with necessary capabilities and regulatory licenses, could operate as the local utility as well, as in the case of provincial utilities in countries such as the US and the Philippines. These cooperative-utilities often set up urban microgrids to reduce their electricity procurement costs, reduce T&D losses, and stabilize their grid.

Community-Owned Model

A community-owned model is similar to the up-front capital investment model and the cooperative-owned model, although it is often deployed for a community of individual retail and/or residential consumers, and typically not for a group of commercial and industrial consumers, as is often the case in cooperative-owned model. This model is also often deployed for rural, remote microgrids and island microgrids in developing countries, to bring access to energy to consumers who would otherwise remain off-grid and unserved or underserved by modern electricity services. These communities of on-grid urban and off-grid rural and/or island consumers are often organized as cooperatives too, although other forms of community organizations, including private limited companies are also structured many times. Up-front capital investment and ownership of microgrid asset would be the responsibility of the local community organization, who would likely carry out the installation through an EPC service provider. These local residential electricity consumers typically come together to organize themselves into a community organization to aggregate their electricity demand, thereby achieving larger scale microgrids that allow cost and operational efficiencies. When the installation is complete, the energy generated from microgrid asset would be supplied to local consumers, who are likely to be members of the community organization that owns and operates the microgrid asset.

Many of these communities often lack the technical and/or financial expertise to design, install, operate, maintain, and manage finances of a microgrid system and hence, require significant technical and/or financial support and training before they are able to manage these systems. This is particularly true for remote and/or island communities where technical and/or financial management skillset(s) are often limited.

Pay-As-You-Go Model

Pay-As-You-Go (PAYG) as a business model emerged a couple of decades ago, through the widespread use of mobile phone technology across the world, wherein prepaid mobile phone credits were introduced as a way to make mobile phone usage affordable, flexible, and accessible to consumers of various income levels and affordability. The same model was adopted to make solar energy products more affordable in the developing world about 7–8 years ago, more commonly in developing countries of Sub-Saharan Africa, and also in countries such as India and Myanmar. Solar product companies realized that, to reach larger sections of their potential market and to achieve high-growth, their products had to be made affordable to the off-grid consumer, by combining consumer finance with the solar product, which banks or MFIs were unwilling to provide at scale. PAYG essentially involves efficiently spreading out the cost of the solar asset over a part of its usage time period—effectively mimicking an off-grid household's energy expenditure patterns, which often involves fossil fuels such as kerosene and diesel. Essentially, PAYG solar models offer lease-to-own or perpetual lease-based payment plans to rural, off-grid consumers, thereby enhancing their affordability. The introduction of the PAYG solution in the rural energy market in developing countries, particularly in the Solar Home Systems (SHS) segment, coincided with the convergence of key technology and financing trends—rapidly falling solar PV and battery prices, significant scale-up in manufacturing base for solar products in countries such as the PRC, rapidly increasing deployment and usage of mobile money services, and crucially, significant amount of seed and growth capital made available by a plethora of equity, debt, and grant providers from around the world.

A typical PAYG prepaid metering and mobile payments technology platform performs the following three tasks: (i) makes it simple and easy to pay, based on a familiar payment model used for prepaid mobile phone top-ups or direct mobile phone-based fee payments; (ii) reduces transaction costs of collecting micro-payments from large number of customers; (iii) mitigates risks for investors and/or banks that provide asset finance and/or consumer finance by offering full transparency into customers, agents and transactions; and (iv) shuts off the system when payments from customers are delayed or stopped.

While the PAYG technology has largely been used for off-grid SHS sales, it has been integrated into microgrids as well as other consumer appliances as well, such as refrigerators, water purifiers, and air conditioners that are being sold on a progressive purchase or lease-to-own plans in many developing countries, thus making these appliances more affordable to low-income consumers, while also offering a relatively secure technology platform to track and collect micro-payments, thereby generating debt investor interest. Several technology providers, such as US-based Angaza Design, offer PAYG technology platform as a stand-alone hardware + software + cloud-based platform to SHS, microgrid, and appliance manufacturers and retailers.

Remote Microgrids (Non-Grid Connected)

Remote rural and island microgrids have been deployed in many countries as a way to bring access to energy to remote rural/island communities that are often unserved or underserved by modern electricity services. While developing countries in Asia have made significant progress in recent years in increasing their rural and household electrification rates—through both extension of national grids and off-grid energy technologies—hundreds of millions of rural and/or remote households and businesses in developing Asia are still without electricity. In some cases where electricity is available, it is often unreliable and insufficient, thereby affecting economic activities in these rural and remote locations. Remote and/or island microgrids represent a cost-effective model to bring reliable and economical electricity to these communities.

Remote and island microgrids have historically been implemented as community-owned models or local utility-owned models. Given that these off-grid microgrids do not have access to grid electricity as an alternative source, they often require battery or energy storage solutions integrated into their systems, thereby increasing their system costs when compared to urban, grid-tied microgrids. In addition, since the electricity consumers in these rural areas are often low-income households with limited electricity demand (at least initially), revenue generation potential is also often low. Hence, historically, many of these remote and island microgrids have been implemented with significant grants and subsidies from governments and development finance institutions such as ADB.

However, commercial remote microgrid models have started to emerge in recent years, with the most prominent one being the Anchor-Business-Consumer (ABC) model of rural microgrids being implemented by RESCOs such as OMC Power in India, Yoma Micropower in Myanmar and Canopy Power in Indonesia and the Philippines. The ABC model essentially resolves the issue of lack of commercial viability of remote microgrids by combining electricity demand from anchor customers such as telecom towers and ecotourism resorts with local business consumers (such as small local shops, agro-processing units, etc.) and local household consumers. The model works well in terms of load management too, since anchor customers have nearly steady load throughout day and night, while business consumers often have their peak demand during the day and household consumers have their peak demand at nighttime. Tariffs are often structured in multiple tiers, so that low-consuming household consumers effectively pay lower tariffs per kWh than high-consuming anchor customers.

Nonetheless, there are several remote locations and islands where such ABC models may not be feasible, due to a lack of anchor and business customers. Often, the minigrids deployed in such locations receive noncommercial capital investments, with revenue collection aimed at recovering at least O&M costs. In such locations, development agencies have started to offer technical assistance and capacity building support, to increase productive uses of energy (PUE), so that increased business activities could lead to additional off-take of energy services offered by the minigrid, and also enable local economic development. The Rockefeller Foundation-supported Smart Power for Rural Development (SPRD) minigrid program in India and Myanmar includes such PUE support offered by the program's development partners.[1]

[1]   Rockefeller Foundation. Smart Power for Rural Development. https://www.rockefellerfoundation.org/our-work/initiatives/smart-power-for-rural-development/.

References

ABB. *GTM Microgrid Paper*. https://library.e.abb.com/public/0356a68f668647599efce1d156ee6c7d/GTM%20 Microgrid%20paper_v4.docx.

———. 2017a. Innovative Business Cases for the Deployment of Microgrids. Presented at the State Energy Conference held in North Carolina. https://d3n8a8pro7vhmx.cloudfront.net/rtcc/pages/44/attachments/ original/1493135223/Microgrids_Panel_Combined_Presentations.pdf?1493135223.

———. 2017b. *ABB Microgrids Case Study—Longmeadow, South Africa*. http://search.abb.com/library/Download.as px?DocumentID=9AKK107045A3118&LanguageCode=en&DocumentPartId=LoRes&Action=Launch.

———. Tam, C.W., ed. 2019. *Urban Microgrids: Enabling Utility and C&I Towards Green Digital Future*. Manila: ADB; Asia Clean Energy Forum 2019.

Allesi, P. L.. *Universal Access to Energy and the Role of Regulation*. https://turinschool.eu/files/turinschool/ISS16_ Alessi.pdf.

Asian Development Bank (ADB). 2017a. *Deployment of Hybrid Renewable Energy Systems in Minigrids*. Manila. https://www.adb.org/documents/deployment-hybrid-renewable-energy-minigrids.

———. 2017b. *Developing Renewable Energy Mini-Grids in Myanmar—A Guidebook*. Manila. https://www.adb.org/sites/ default/files/institutional-document/391606/developing-renewable-mini-grids-myanmar-guidebook.pdf.

———. 2017c. *Improving Lives of Rural Communities Through Developing Small Hybrid Renewable Energy Systems*. Manila. https://www.adb.org/documents/improving-lives-rural-communities-hybrid-renewable-energy.

ADB. 2017d. *Microsoft Excel-Based Tool Kit for Planning Hybrid Energy Systems: A User Guide*. Manila. https://www. adb.org/documents/microsoft-excel-based-tool-kit-hybrid-energy-systems-guide.

———. 2018. *Handbook on Battery Energy Storage System*. Manila. https://www.adb.org/sites/default/files/ publication/479891/handbook-battery-energy-storage-system.pdf.

———. 2019. *Guidebook for Deploying Distributed Renewable Energy Systems: A Case Study on the Cobrador Hybrid Solar PV Mini-Grid*. Manila. https://www.adb.org/publications/deploying-distributed-renewable-energy- systems-guidebook.

Anam, F., A. A. Sahito, and A. Shah. 2018. *Comparison of AC and DC Microgrid Considering Solar-Wind Hybrid Renewable Energy System. Engineering Science and Technology International Research Journal*. 2(1). pp. 33–38. http://www.estirj.com/Volume.1/6Faiza21.pdf.

Arup. 2019. *Five-Minute Guide to Microgrids*. https://www.arup.com/perspectives/publications/promotional- materials/section/five-minute-guide-to-microgrids.

Black and Veatch, 2016. *Microgrid Design & Execution Handbook: A consistent project approach for reliable results*. Black and Veatch. Kansas, USA.

Brattle Group. 2019. *Additional Transmission Investment Needed to Cost-Effectively Support Growth of Electrification in North America.* https://www.brattle.com/news-and-knowledge/news/brattle-economists-additional-transmission-investment-needed-to-cost-effectively-support-growth-of-electrification-in-north-america.

California Energy Commission. 2018. *Microgrid Analysis and Case Studies Report.* https://ww2.energy.ca.gov/2018publications/CEC-500-2018-022/CEC-500-2018-022.pdf.

Devi, P. and M. Babu. 2017. Implementation of Proportional Power Sharing in Hierarchical Droop Control for Reactive Power Sharing in Microgrid. *International Journal of Advanced Research in Electrical Electronics and Instrumentation Engineering.* 6(2). pp. 642–652. http://www.ijareeie.com/upload/2017/february/26_REACTIVE_JOURNAL.pdf.

Elizondo, L.R., ed. 2018. *Solar Energy: Integration of Photovoltaic Systems in Microgrids.* Delft: Delft University of Technology (TU Delft). https://ocw.tudelft.nl/courses/solar-energy-integration-photovoltaic-systems-microgrids/.

Energy4Impact (previously known as GVEP International). 2014. *Financing Mini-Grids in East Africa.* https://www.german-energy-solutions.de/GES/Redaktion/DE/Publikationen/ Praesentationen/2015/2015-03-19-iv-mini-grids-03-gvep.pdf?__blob=publicationFile&v=9.

Environmental Protection Agency (EPA). *Energy Efficiency for Water Utilities.* https://www.epa.gov/sustainable-water-infrastructure/energy-efficiency-water-utilities.

Ett, Rachel. 2018. *Reality Check: Blockchain Needs Proof of Concept Before Revolutionizing the Grid.* https://www.greentechmedia.com/articles/read/reality-check-blockchain-needs-proof-of-concept-before-revolutionizing-the.

EU-India Technical Cooperation Energy. http://www.pvrooftop.in/programme_info/05_business.htm.

Faisal, M. and S. B. Islam. 2017. *Planning, Operation, and Protection of Microgrids: An Overview. Energy Procedia* (107). pp. 94–100. https://doi.org/10.1016/j.egypro.2016.12.137.

George, S. and S. Chauhan. 2015. An Investigation into Centralized and Decentralized Micro-Grid Systems with Synchronization Capability and Flywheel. *International Journal of Enhanced Research in Science Technology & Engineering.* 4(5). pp. 225–248. https://pdfs.semanticscholar.org/068b/e24d624ddfe09e4043deeac2ea72c6655499.pdf.

Ghasempour, A. 2019. Internet of Things in Smart Grid: Architecture, Applications, Services, Key Technologies, and Challenges. *Inventions.* 4(22). doi:doi:10.3390/inventions4010022.

Giraldez, J. et al. 2018. *Phase I Microgrid Cost Study: Data Collection and Analysis of Microgrid Costs in the United States.* National Renewable Energy Laboratory (NREL), Juwi Americas, and Navigant Consulting. www.nrel.gov/publications.

GreenTech Media (GTM). 2014. *Microgrids 2014 and Beyond: The Evolution of Localized Energy Optimization.* GridEdge, GTM.

HDBaker & Company. 2016a. *What are the Components of a Microgrid?* https://www.hdbaker.com/article/what-are-the-components-of-a-microgrid-.

———. 2016b. *What are the Value Propositions for Microgrids?* http://www.hdbaker.com/article/what-are-the-value-propositions-for-microgrids-.

Hirose, K., J. T. Reilly, and H. Irie. 2013. *The Sendai Microgrid Operational Experience in the Aftermath of the Tohoku Earthquake: A Case Study. New Energy and Industrial Technology Development Organization (NEDO).* https://www.nedo.go.jp/content/100516763.pdf.

Honghua, X. 2015. *Status and Challenges of Micro-Grid Demonstration in China*. https://events.development.asia/system/files/materials/2015/05/201505-status-and-challenges-microgrid-demonstration-china.pdf.

Howitt, Mark. 2018. *Gigawatt Scale Storage for Gigawatt Scale Renewables. Journal of Energy and Power Engineering*, Vol. 12. https://www.researchgate.net/publication/325622672_Gigawatt_Scale_Storage_for_Gigawatt_Scale_Renewables.

Iansiti, M. and K. Lakhani. 2017. The Truth About Blockchain. *Harvard Business Review*. 95(1). pp. 118–127. https://hbr.org/2017/01/the-truth-about-blockchain.

Justo, J. J. and F. Mwasilu. 2013. *AC-Microgrids versus DC-Microgrids with Distributed Energy Resources: A Review. Renewable and Sustainable Energy Reviews*. https://www.researchgate.net/publication/270831774.

Kawahara, T., ed. 2019. Distributed Renewable Energy in Emerging Countries. ADB workshop papers. Tokyo: Bloomberg New Energy Finance.

Lawrence Berkeley National Laboratory (LBNL). 2019. *About Microgrids*. Microgrids at Berkeley Lab. https://building-microgrid.lbl.gov/about-microgrids-0.

Li, G. et al. 2016. HELOS: Heterogeneous Load Scheduling for Electric Vehicle-Integrated Microgrids. *IEEE Transactions on Vehicular Technology*. PP(99). https://www.researchgate.net/publication/311502708_HELOS_Heterogeneous_Load_Scheduling_for_Electric_Vehicle-Integrated_Microgrids/stats.

Lilienthal, P. 2018. *Microgrid Value Propositions Revisited: Part One*. Homer Microgrid News. https://microgridnews.com/microgrid-value-propositions-revisited-part-one/.

Metropolitan Water District of Southern California (MWDH), US. *Solar Power: Metropolitan's Investment in Renewable Energy*. http://www.mwdh2o.com/PDF_NewsRoom/solar_7%2025%20final.pdf.

Microgrid Institute. 2014. *About Microgrids*. http://www.microgridinstitute.org/microgrid-background.html.

Microgrid Resources Coalition (MRC). 2017. *Microgrid Features*. https://www.districtenergy.org/microgrids/about-microgrids97/features.

Nandapawar, H. 2018. *Blockchain—Smart Disruption for Clean Energy Deployment*. Manila: ADB; Asia Clean Energy Forum 2018.

Navigant Consulting. 2017. Non-Wires Alternatives: Nontraditional Transmission and Distribution Solutions. Navigant Research.

Navigant Consulting. 2018. Are Non-Wires Solutions the Next Big Thing? In GWikler, G. et al. eds. AESP Magazine. *Navigant Research*. https://www.navigant.com/-/media/www/site/downloads/energy/2018/pages-from-aesp-magazine-2018navigantarticle.pdf.

Organisation for Economic Co-operation and Development (OECD). 2019. *Blockchain Technologies as a Digital Enabler for Sustainable Infrastructure*. OECD Directorate for Financial and Enterprise Affairs.

Planas, E. et al. 2015. AC and DC Technology in Microgrids: A Review. *Renewable and Sustainable Energy Reviews*. 43: pp. 726–749. https://doi.org/10.1016/j.rser.2014.11.067

Romankiewic, J., et al. 2013. *International Microgrid Assessment: Governance, Incentives, and Experience (IMAGINE)*. The European Council for an Energy-Efficient Economy's 2013 Summer Study on Energy Efficiency. European Council for an Energy-Efficient Economy. http://eta-publications.lbl.gov/sites/default/files/imagine-eceee.pdf.

S&C Electric. 2018. *The Long- and Short-Term Care of Your Microgrid*. https://www.sandc.com/globalassets/sac-electric/documents/sharepoint/documents---all-documents/educational-material-180-4506.pdf?dt=637212583873651116.

Sabzehgar, R. 2017. Overview of Technical Challenges, Available Technologies, and Ongoing Developments of AC/DC Microgrids. In W.P. Cao, and J. Yang, *Development and Integration of Microgrids*. doi:10.5772/intechopen.69400.

Samad, T., et. al. 2016. *Automated Demand Response for Smart Buildings and Microgrids: The State of the Practice and Research Challenges*. Proceedings of the Institute of Electrical and Electronics Engineers. 104(4). pp. 726–744. doi:10.1109/JPROC.2016.2520639.

Santos, A. Q., et al. 2018. Framework for Microgrid Design Using Social, Economic, and Technical Analysis. *Energies*. 11: 2832. doi:10.3390/en11102832. https://www.mdpi.com/1996-1073/11/10/2832.

Scauzillo, S. 2016. Metropolitan Water District: Saving Money Lost during Drought by Investing in Solar. *San Gabriel Valley Tribune*. 10 August 2016. Updated: 30 August 2017. https://www.sgvtribune.com/2016/08/10/metropolitan-water-district-saving-money-lost-during-drought-by-investing-in-solar/.

Schneider Electric. 2016. *How Microgrids Contribute to the Energy Transition*. https://sun-connect-news.org/fileadmin/DATEIEN/Dateien/New/9982095_12-01-16A_EN.pdf.

Scott, N. 2016. *Microgrids: A Guide to their Issues and Value. Highlands and Islands Enterprise in Partnership with the Government of Scotland*. https://www.hie.co.uk/media/5957/a-guide-to-microgrids.pdf.

Shahnia, F., et al. 2014. Interconnected Autonomous Microgrids in Smart Grids with Self-Healing. In J. Hossain and A. Mahmud, eds. *Renewable Energy Integration, Challenges and Solutions*. Singapore: Springer Singapore. https://eprints.qut.edu.au/69798/.

Smart Electric Power Alliance (SEPA). 2019. *Transactive Energy: Real World Applications for the Modern Grid*. https://sepapower.org/resource/transactive-energy-real-world-applications-for-the-grid/.

Souche, A. 2014. *Financing of Clean Energy Projects in Southeast Asia: Challenges and Opportunities*. Renewable Energy World Asia 2014. https://www.dfdl.com/wp-content/uploads/2014/10/dfdl%20financing%20of%20clean%20energy%20projects%20in%20south%20east%20asia%20%20challenges%20and%20opportunities.pdf.

Strahl, J., E. Paris, and L. Vogel, L. 2015. *The Bankable Microgrid: Strategies for Financing On-Site Power Generation*. Navigant Consulting. https://www.navigant.com/-/media/www/site/downloads/energy/2015/powergen_bankablemicrogrid_dec2015.pdf.

The Metropolitan Water District of Southern California. 2016. *Solar Power: Metropolitan's Investment in Renewable Energy*. http://www.mwdh2o.com/PDF_NewsRoom/solar_7%2025%20final.pdf.

Thurstan, C., ed. 2018. *Microgrid Cybersecurity Tightens with Standards Adoption. CleanTechnica*. https://cleantechnica.com/2018/12/26/microgrid-cybersecurity-tightens-with-standards-adoption/.

Wanshan Archipelago. *The Wanshan Archipelago: Wikipedia*. https://en.wikipedia.org/wiki/Wanshan_Archipelago.

Wood MacKenzie Power and Renewables. 2019. *Microgrid Market Overview*. https://www.greentechmedia.com/webinars/webinar/at-the-edge-of-the-grid-best-practices-in-utility-digitalization-and-busine.

World Business Council for Sustainable Development (WBCSD). 2017. *Microgrids for Commercial and Industrial Companies*. https://www.wbcsd.org/Programs/Climate-and-Energy/Energy/REscale/Resources/Microgrids-for-commercial-and-industrial-companies.

Zhang, F. 2019. *In the Dark: How Much Do Power Sector Distortions Cost South Asia*. Washington, DC: The World Bank.

Zhou, J. et al. 2019. Design and Analysis of Flexible Multi-Microgrid Interconnection Scheme for Mitigating Power Fluctuation and Optimizing Storage Capacity. *Energies*. 12:2132. doi:10.3390/en12112132.

www.ingramcontent.com/pod-product-compliance
Lightning Source LLC
Chambersburg PA
CBHW051656210326
41518CB00026B/2607